THE BIGGEST
SHOW IN TOWN

THE BIGGEST
SHOW IN TOWN

RECORD OF THE INTERNATIONAL
EXHIBITION, DUBLIN 1907

KEN FINLAY

NONSUCH

First published 2007

Nonsuch Publishing
73 Lower Leeson Street
Dublin 2, Ireland
www.nonsuch-publishing.com

British Library Cataloguing in Publication Data.
A catalogue record for this book is available from the British Library.

ISBN 978 1 84588 579 3

Typesetting and origination by NPI Media Group
Printed in Great Britain

CONTENTS

Acknowledgements

Many people helped in the creation of this book. The staff of the Irish Architectural Archive, Dublin City Library and Archive (formerly the Gilbert Library), Dún Laoghaire Library (where a chance find in the archive section started me on the search) and the National Photographic Archive were all unfailingly helpful. The online Irish Newspaper Archive also proved a great resource when tracking down the last few niggling details. James O'Brien of the Collectors' Shop, Blackrock Market, and Declan O'Kelly of Cathedral Stamps, very kindly allowed me to scan some of their postcards which were beyond my budget. Finally, this book would never have seen the light of day but for the extraordinary patience of Anne who put up with the clutter and the very time-consuming work. Sincere thanks to you all!

INTRODUCTION

In 1907 the Irish International Exhibition was the talk of the town; a century later Dubliners have only the vaguest idea that it ever happened, and many are particularly surprised to learn that Herbert Park, rather than the nearby RDS, was the venue.

Most people have, however, seen some photographs of the Exhibition – even if they weren't completely sure what it was they were seeing. The great number of postcards by Tallon (who had actually paid the organisers for, he thought, the sole privilege), Hely, Lawrence and others, turn up regularly on eBay – with some exceptions they can be bought for a few euro.

The official record and catalogue, edited by W.E. Dennehy and published by Hely's Ltd, Dublin, is a rare and expensive volume but can be found in several of the city libraries.

Apart from this introduction, all of the information in this book is drawn from the above texts. The photographs vary; some are from the same sources, others from an illustrated brochure drawn up by the Exhibition organisers to encourage exhibitors and advertisers, and some photographs and postcards are from my own collection.

The official record paints an accurate, if somewhat sanitised and upbeat, account of the Irish International Exhibition, from the initial 1903 articles by W.E. Dennehy, editor of the *Irish Independent*, to the final liquidators' accounts of 31 August 1909. This introduction complements that book and dwells in more detail on those areas which the Exhibition organisers, for one reason or another, decided to erase from their history.

Missing, in particular, is any report on the 'detractors' of the Exhibition, or their reasons for doing so (some typical denunciations are discussed later). It is hardly surprising, however, that the organisers felt little need to expound on the theories advanced by those who were opposed to the Exhibition.

An advertisement for the International Exhibition of 4 May 1907.

Perhaps of more interest is the lack of any explanation, beyond bad weather, for the Exhibition's lack of commercial success – in the winding-up process sixty-four of the guarantors paid out a total of £45,226.

But weather did play a part, and as such it stretches the boundary of belief that the organisers didn't factor in the Irish weather, and that no one seems to have challenged them on it. The Exhibition was heavily reliant on outdoor events and yet, during the six months, little or no effort was made to move attractions indoors when the weather was bad.

So why did the Exhibition fall short of making a profit, or even breaking even? It is my opinion that the cost of entry and separate charges for popular sideshows pushed the Exhibition beyond the means of the vast majority of ordinary workers. This, the organisers freely admitted, was a deliberate decision, made to attract the right kind of visitors. The average cost per individual can be estimated from reports of groups of workers, who had been given 5s by their employers to cover their day at the Exhibition.

Halfway through the six months of the Exhibition, the admission price (1s per adult, and 6d per child) was reduced after 6 p.m. in an attempt to boost night-time attendance. The definition of 'child' was also extended from twelve years to fifteen. By early August, it is clear that Sundays in particular were not busy (whether for religious or other reasons is not clear) and Sunday-opening was stopped; 'as the class of people for whose benefit the Exhibition was opened on Sundays are not availing themselves of the advantages, it will not in future be open on that day', reported the Finance and General Purposes Committee. (*Irish Independent*, 8 August)

Admission prices were reduced further in October, and this time the advertisements were quite clear in stating that it was to encourage the 'artisan' and 'working class' to attend. One anonymous *Irish Times* reader noted that, while he thought it a great idea to encourage the attendance of the working classes, in his experience the price change brought the wrong sort of people to the Exhibition, definitely not the class of people he would associate with.

In addition, many of the sideshows were not exactly a novelty – some, including the Somali Village, and the Water chute, had previously appeared at other exhibitions. Even an enthusiastic *Irish Independent* reporter, presumably under orders not to have a single negative in his report, found the 'wow' factor somewhat lacking. The sideshows, while proving financially beneficial to the organisers of the Exhibition, seemed to have been something of an embarrassment and are barely mentioned in the official documentation.

An impartial reading of the official account shows serious-minded people tackling a large project with little time (and even less inclination) to spend on trying to think up ways of entertaining the masses.

It should be taken into account that the Exhibition didn't actually need to make a profit, it just had to avoid losing more than the £168,000 put up by the guarantors. Many of those who put up large guarantees also owned hotels, railways and other businesses, which made large sums from the Exhibition, so it is not unreasonable to say that what they lost on the swings, they more than made up for on the roundabouts.

OPPOSITION TO THE EXHIBITION

The selections below outline the views held by those opposed to the Irish International Exhibition, before, during and at the end. It is interesting to note that there were almost always dissenting views at these meetings and the decisions often came after a close vote.

The proposed Irish International Exhibition was the subject of debate by Meath County Council in early 1905. The chairman, Mr John Sweetman, proposed that the council should pass a resolution of disapproval in line with that proposed by the Coisde Gnotha of the Gaelic League (that it would injure the revival of Irish industries, and that the next Dublin Exhibition should be one of Irish exhibits alone).

The motion was opposed by Mr Kennedy:

> He had considerable sympathy with the objects of the Gaelic League in so far as he considered those objects were practicable and did not come into conflict with the national interests of the country … The question was: what would bring more money into the country? Would they have more people coming to look at a national than an international exhibition? Would the people who were now subscribing and guaranteeing a large sum of money to start an international exhibition be prepared to put down money for a national exhibition? Would the people who drew the red herring across the path of a useful enterprise stump down the necessary funds for even a national exhibition? For his part he did not believe it … If, as many people believed, Ireland was many years behind the average of other countries in commercial and industrial activity, was it by looking in on themselves, by looking back on a long list of failures, they were to advance the country, or by looking outside, by taking their stand among the nations of the earth, and learning from what they saw in the progress of other

countries having greater advantages than they had, the way which lay the course of future education and advancement by this country. In his view it was obvious that the advantage lay in looking outwards.

Mr McKenna elaborated on these concerns:

Unfortunately in this country most of them had a taste for foreign things and sent their money to the strangers without receiving anything in return but imported goods. It would be unfair to bring those foreigners into competition with their own manufacturers who were not supported by their people as they ought to be. A section of the people of Ireland actually boycotted the Irish manufacturers ... He agreed that they had a great deal to learn from the foreigner, but it was another thing to bring him in to compete with their Industries. At a time when their own manufacturers were not receiving all the support they deserved it would be an act of folly to start an inter-national exhibition. They should rather assist such industries as they had in their own country.

Lt Col Everard said ... it was perfectly clear that a national exhibition at the present moment would be a little premature. It would be, in his opinion, at least, because they had not had time to show what could be done by restoring some of their lost industries. At the same time if the Exhibition was to be held as early as 1906 he thought an exhibition confined to national products could possibly attract the attention of the world. It was almost impossible such an exhibition could be made to pay. There was a great deal to be said for the holding of an inter-national exhibition because a great many of the products of this country could well bear comparison with anything the world could produce, and why should they be afraid to put them in competition with the productions of other countries? Not many of them had travelled in foreign countries, and surely it was an advantage to see what other countries could produce.

The chairman: are we going to collect the general public of Ireland to induce them to spend money on foreign goods just because some half dozen, or dozen, or two dozen manufacturers might have their eyes opened by seeing some of those foreign goods. It is their business if there is a demand on Irish goods to go abroad to these exhibitions ... instead of trying or rather succeeding in injuring the trade and manufactures of Ireland by collecting in to Ireland all the goods of the rest of the world for the sake of a few men to learn the business; I do not think that would be wise.

The motion was carried by ten votes to nine, with one abstention. (*Meath Chronicle*, 5 March 1904)

The following year Mr Sweetman had not changed his beliefs:

At the annual meeting of the General Council of the Irish County Councils, held in City Hall yesterday [12 January 1905], under the presidency of Sir Thomas Esmonde

… Mr Sweetman brought forward a resolution which declared that the proposed International Exhibition would be most detrimental to their wish that Irish-manufactured goods should be alone used in Ireland, and requested any patriotic Irishmen who have advocated such an Exhibition to withdraw their support from it, and, on the other hand, to support the holding of a national exhibition, in order that the public may see what can be produced in Ireland, and may be induced to demand of the shopkeepers that in future home manufactures be pushed in their shops, instead of foreign goods, as is done at present.

Mr Cullinan, MP, seconded the motion. Mr Joseph Mooney, JP, said he was one of those who believed if they had any Exhibition at all that an International Exhibition would be the best, as they could learn something of the manufactures of other countries. There was underlying all this opposition to the International Exhibition an admission of weakness in regard to Irish products. If they were not afraid of competition what injury could be done by putting their goods side by side with foreign products? Some of the gentlemen now opposed to the International Exhibition were at first its strongest supports, such as the Lord Mayor, the ex-Lord Mayor, and Mr Dawson, and he was at a loss to know what occurred to make those gentlemen change their opinions. Mr Dawson said there was an attempt to put Irish products in the background; but there was nothing of the sort. The Irish goods were to be placed in the forefront.

Over £160,000 had been subscribed by people for the International project, and he would like to know how much had been subscribed for the national exhibition. Believing that the larger exhibition would embrace the smaller, he refused to abandon the position he had taken up, and he must vote against Mr Sweetman's resolution.

These remarks were supported by Mr Reynolds (Louth) and Mr Crozier, JP (Dublin), who said if the International Exhibition was allowed to go on, it would give employment to hundreds of thousands of men in Dublin.

Mr Byrne (Louth) considered that an International Exhibition would induce an enormous number of people to come amongst them – much more than a purely local one, and, besides, it would show to strangers that Ireland could produce better goods than their own countries.

Mr McDonnell (Galway) sarcastically remarked that the 'Exhibition' was going on already, as they were making an exhibition of themselves. Many of those, he said, who were supporting an International Exhibition, did so for the purpose of getting royalty over here in order to get titles. The time might arrive when King Edward might be invited to open a national exhibition and a native Parliament.

Mr Ryan (Tipperary) thought it would be cowardly not to express an opinion on the matter. He was in favour of a national exhibition.

On a division Mr Sweetman's resolution was adopted by 12 to 5. (*Irish Independent*, Friday 13 January 1905)

The Irish Builder and Engineer (4 May 1907), refers briefly to the opposition:

> At the present moment the whole atmosphere of Dublin is charged with the forthcoming Exhibition; the published Press, the advertisement hoardings, and the conversation of the man in the street are all significant of the near approach of the opening day, to which every Irishman may look forward with some degree of pride. Since the idea of holding an International Exhibition was first formulated, the promoters have had to run the gauntlet of the severest criticism, some of which was justifiable, but much of which was engendered by narrow-minded hostility. Doubtless, in many cases a little more tact on the part of the authorities would have smoothed over the friction that certain lines of policy created … methods have been adopted by the executive which have been extremely difficult for the onlooker to comprehend. But the policy has now reached achievement, its crowning feature, and all concerned are entitled to congratulation.

Even as the Exhibition opened, there were those who remained implacably opposed. On Monday 6 May 1907, the quarterly meeting of the Limerick branch of the Gaelic League returned to the subject:

> Mr D. Meany, Teacher of History in the Classes said … that undertaking [the International Exhibition] had been regarded by all branches of the Gaelic League, and by most public bodies in Ireland as of an anti-national character, and work calculated to give a new lease of life to popular foreign manufacture in this country. It was now acknowledged by everybody, except those who were not the friends of the Revival movement, that this Exhibition, instead of stimulating Irish trade and industry, would have the opposite effect of crippling them. Speaking generally, the County Councils of Ireland had held this view, and as far as the rank and file of the people were concerned, it might be taken that they are dead against it. It had been condemned throughout the country as inimical to the best interests of Ireland during the progress of preparations for it; and now the Exhibition had been opened, in order to give effect to their previous view and decisions, he thought they ought to impress upon their members and all whom they could influence, the desirability of giving the Exhibition a wide berth, and refusing to support it by their presence. He had no doubt but the Exhibition would be very well supported, but they, at least, should not attend it, and he hoped there would be an understanding to that effect amongst the members of their branch (applause) … The views of Mr Meany were adopted by the meeting. (*Evening Telegraph*, Tuesday 7 May 1907)

A lengthy report in the *Evening Telegraph* in early June began with a consideration of the importance, or lack of it, placed upon the Irish element of the Exhibition:

> The Home Industries Section of the International Exhibition is the only department of the undertaking which may be said to have anything distinctively Irish about it;

but it falls very short, indeed, of what a similar section would be were it organised on distinctly Irish national lines, and were helped by the labours of those who have been prominently identified with the national industrial movement. One would imagine that even in an Irish International Exhibition special prominence would be given to a section which was devoted to existing or prospective Irish industries; but it is not so in this case. The section is located in an obscure quarter of the grounds behind the lake, and the Industrial Halls, small in dimensions and uninteresting in their style, are entirely dwarfed by the imposing architecture of the buildings in which the general exhibits are placed and those which are confined to the display of the industries and resources of particular countries. The 'Home' Industries Section is rather a misnomer, because there are included for exhibition in the section not only articles made in the homes of the people, but also the products of factories and workshops. The general effect of the section must be to give the foreign visitor a very inadequate idea, indeed, of the position of Irish industries at the present moment. Had there been an Irish sec-tion in the Exhibition, located in a handsome building occupying a prominent site, in which there would be displayed all kinds of Irish industries and manufactures, with a department attached devoted to a display of those goods which are not now made in Ireland, but for the manufacture of which the country is suitable, the effect on the mind of the foreign visitor and on the people of this country visiting the Exhibition would be much more striking, and the results more likely to be satisfactory. As it is, the industries of Ireland are scattered in different departments; and, in fact, Ireland is represented at the Irish International Exhibition as a province, and a somewhat obscure province at that, instead of being, as she rightly claims to be – a Nation. (*Evening Telegraph*, 3 June 1907)

The Port and Docks Board meeting of 17 October, discussing their possible involve-ment in the Exhibition should it continue into 1908, saw Lord Mayor of Dublin, Joseph Patrick Nanetti, hitherto silent on the subject, declare his views on the Irish International Exhibition:

> It was, in a sense, a good Exhibition, but he heard also on all sides that it had done no good for the trade of the city. The city hotel and restaurant proprietors complained that they had lost money by the Exhibition, and it would be a serious matter to ask a Board to sanction the proposal before the meeting.

He was joined by Mr Hutchinson who said, 'he had heard nothing but complaints by hotel and restaurant keepers of the injury that had been done them by the Exhibition – that as the public got good and cheap luncheons at the Exhibition they stayed there. People said their business had been injured.'

Several other Board members disagreed, among them Mr North, proprietor of two hotels (Sackville Street and Westland Row) who noted, 'owing to the Exhibition they had doubled their business. In fact, they never had a year like it before.'

The Lord Mayor can hardly have been surprised when the *Irish Independent* turned the heat on him. He had, after all, been notably absent from the official opening.

The following Tuesday the paper carried a letter from James Clements, Director, Switzers:

> Our attention has been called to the speech made by the Lord Mayor of Dublin at the meeting of the Port and Docks Board, in which he stated that he had been informed in one or two large houses in Grafton Street that they had been injured by the Exhibition. As this might lead to misapprehension as regards our opinion on the matter, we beg to say that our experience is quite the contrary. It is, of course, very difficult to tell exactly the results, as the buying is chiefly done in Grafton Street but, from the large numbers of important orders which we can trace directly to the Exhibition, and from the large increase in our trade for the half year, we can come to no other conclusion than that the Exhibition has been of very considerable benefit to us.

It was followed a few days later by another letter from Mr Clements in which he noted that his only intention in writing the first letter was to, 'do justice to an undertaking which, in concept and execution is undoubtedly a credit to Dublin and to save a possible misapprehension which might arise from the Lord Mayor's ambiguous reference to shops in Grafton Street'.

The *Independent* noted that the members of the Hotel and Tourist Association had decided to write to the Lord Mayor intimating that he 'had been misinformed with regard to the effect of the Exhibition on the hotels and restaurants of Dublin; that the hotels and restaurants had not suffered loss, but, on the contrary they benefited very considerably by the Exhibition'.

The Hotel and Tourist Association also approved of the holding of the Exhibition for the coming year.

Mr W. Rippingale, Harcourt Street, in drawing the attention of the Hotel and Tourist Association meeting to the Lord Mayor's statement, expressed the opinion that there was not a hotel in Dublin that had not benefited to an exceptional extent by the International Exhibition.

> They must have doubled their receipts … and some of them even went beyond that. I have met many people interested in hotels in Dublin, during the season, and in every case I was assured personally that they were doing an enormous trade. Personally, I may say that during the few months of the Exhibition we ourselves trebled our business, and on an average had to send thirty or forty customers away every night. Not only have the hotels done an increased trade; but the butcher and the grocer also benefited. In fact, the general trade of the city must have benefited to an enormous extent. From fifteen to twenty parcels came into our premises each day from different traders in the town, for people stopping at our place, and we found it necessary to appoint a boy to allocate the parcels to the different rooms.

Mr Rippingale admitted that the hotels and restaurants suffered somewhat in the early weeks of the Exhibition, but he had reason to state that they had recovered from their loss afterwards. The fact that a million people must have come into Dublin during the season meant an enormous amount of trade for the city. The publicans and the tobacconists had suffered more or less; but, after all, they were a rather small proportion of the traders of Dublin. He thought that the hotel and restaurant proprietors should pass a strong resolution taking exception to the statements of the Lord Mayor and Councillor Hutchinson. The Association, as an association, ought also to move a resolution in support of the extension of the Exhibition to next year. He was speaking to a leading member of the Exhibition Committee, who was also a member of the Pembroke Urban Council, and that gentleman assured him that the matter would go through, and that there would be attractions at Ballsbridge next year that were unknown to the committee during the past season.

'I think the Lord Mayor had a good deal of cheek,' remarked Mr McCoy, 'in never having put his foot inside the Exhibition, and then making sweeping statements at the Port and Docks Board that led the people to believe that the hotels and restaurants lost by the Exhibition.'

A resolution embodying the above-mentioned decision was then adopted. The *Independent* wrote:

> If the Lord Mayor of Dublin has not sufficient sense of personal responsibility to cause him to weigh his words when speaking in public, he might confer with prudent friends as to what is becoming the dignity of the honourable office of which he is the incumbent. His random statements at the last meeting of the Port and Docks Board with reference to the effects of the Exhibition on trade in the city were contradicted on the spot, and still stronger denials have since been forthcoming … The experience of the citizens of every class will supply instances of benefits conferred upon Dublin by the holding of the Exhibition. To say that the traders of the city gained nothing by the enormous influx of visitors attracted by the Exhibition is so utterly at variance with readily ascertainable facts as to be inexcusable on the plea of ignorance and indefensible on any other. The Lord Mayor used to speak with some pride of being the first representative of Labour to fill the chair. He seems to have lost touch during his second year of office with working-class opinion in the city, else he would not have hazarded the reckless mis-statement he made in his speech at the meeting of the Port and Docks Board.

The Meath Chronicle marked the end of the Exhibition with a particularly vitriolic editorial:

> The International Exhibition, which closed on Saturday last, had, long before that interesting event in its brief career, ceased to be taken seriously by the country. In fact,

its history justified, if justification were necessary, the criticisms and hostility that the project met when first proposed. It has led to large sums of money being sent out of Ireland; and one of its most elaborate features – the Canadian Section – was avowedly pushed to encourage emigration to the Dominion wildernesses.

A few Dublin traders and hotel-keepers may have benefited; a few carrying companies may have enjoyed enhanced receipts, but the bulk of the increased traffic done was confined to the country itself; and, as always happens on such occasions, when the stimulus is removed, increased economies in this direction will bring receipts to their normal figures in the few years to follow. In any case, exhibitions, even International Exhibitions, are not intended to fill the pockets of railway and tramway company's shareholders, nor to give city hotels big returns.

Nor, indeed, was the description 'international' deserved. There were objects on exhibit from foreign parts, no doubt, and notably Italian firms cornered more orders than otherwise they would have been likely to get in many years. But in the true sense of the term, there was no exhibition of the wares and processes which make other nations prosperous. Nor was there any need for a display of the kind in Ireland. As was said when the project of holding an exhibition was mooted a few years ago, and said with truth, every leading street in our great towns is an 'International Exhibition'. Not a shop but has its goods from all and every land, except, frequently, its own. Foreign makers were not blind to the facts of the case; they did not rush into needless expense in paying big rents for stalls at Ballsbridge when their gents were kept busy enough 'bagging' orders in plenty from shopkeepers in every corner of the country. And such wares as were put on view, if they did anything at all, served merely to belittle the Irish products also in evidence.

What, then, was the true function performed by this Exhibition, which was reared in opposition to all that was best and most intelligent in Irish public opinion? Briefly and plainly it was what has come to be known as a variety show. This character it assumed from the first and maintained to the last closing scene of rowdyism which marked its close. Regal, Viceregal, and castle patronage divided with vulgarism of the most objectionable type, the honour of branding the great Ballsbridge Exhibition with its distinguishing mark. This brand is not to disappear. Even at present the proposal to perpetuate it is under discussion, and if the Exhibition which was to do so much for the nation, but failed, does not live a little longer as a gigantic 'peep-show', it will not be the fault of an enterprising band of speculators who have with a clear instinct gauged the situation accurately. Probably guarantees will not be forthcoming so readily for this as for the other more specious ends, which was lavishly exploited twelve months ago. Traders will not put their hands into their pockets to give city boys and girls and their country friends an opportunity for disporting themselves 'on the cheap'. In a sense it would be regrettable for the proposed extension not to be made. It has the merit of plain sailing to plead. The old flag of exploiting the nation has been hauled down; and for the new one there is more justification. But whatever its future may be, there is every reason to expect that the so-called Exhibition will have unpleasant memories for the guarantors; with whom there will be, we suspect, few honest sympathisers. Public opinion must sometimes vindicate itself, even in Ireland. (*The Meath Chronicle*, 16 November 1907)

The 'rowdyism' referred to above was unique, for the previous six months the police had little to do; their inability to control even as large a crowd as 200 over a period of four hours is inexplicable.

The closing of the Irish International Exhibition on Saturday night was marked by scenes of disgraceful rowdyism. A large body of young men, said to be students, assembled at eight o'clock in the vicinity of the open-air bandstand. They had in their possession an all but unlimited supply of crackers and squibs. They were apparently led by an individual who sported a Turkish fez, while another of the gang waved aloft a Union Jack, which was attached to a walking stick. They made their way to the Helter-skelter Lighthouse. Some of them got on it and blocked the apparatus. Their comrades at this time were busily engaged in smashing the electric globes. A number of the rioters proceeded to the Somali Village, caught a man, hoisted him shoulder-high, and vociferously shouted to him to make a speech on technical education and other subjects; but he managed to escape. The rowdies soon afterwards endeavoured to mount the hobby horses, but were sent to the right-about by the men in charge. The switchback railway was next stormed, the disturbers running up and down the tracks, several of them standing on adjacent turnstiles. They next divided themselves into several parties, and ran wildly through the grounds, letting off squibs, cheering and bellowing. Many crackers and squibs were thrown at police, who formed into cordons, with the object of breaking the disturbers up into smaller groups. All this time the Entrance Hall was a scene of almost indescribable uproar. The police, who exhibited great forbearance, at last rushed on the rowdies, and made an arrest. This gave rise to yet further commotion. The disturbers strenuously opposed the constables, who again charged them. They struck out left and right with their clenched hands, and in a few minutes scattered the rioters in all directions. The Central Hall was the next object of the attention of the mob. Here they massed to the number of close on two hundred, indulging in catcalls, shrieks, and every variety of shouting. Ultimately they took possession of the bandstand. The police most vigorously intervened. They scaled the platform, and as a result of a fierce tussle, the invaders were hurled off. But the latter were determined to be avenged for the repulse which they had had. They tore the bark coverings off the pillars, and fusilladed the police with them. However, they were once more routed. The rowdies were not by any means overawed. They next surged to the open-air bandstand, and leaped up on it, seized a man, placed him on a chair, and hurled him over the stand. They then commenced to smash the chairs, and threw them and ignited squibs at the people. The police again charged them and threw them off the stand. The rowdies then retreated to the Grand Central Hall. Once more they invaded the bandstand, and again they were ejected by the Constables. Ireland's Own band was playing at the time, but were unable, owing to the exciting events which occurred, to go through the programme which had been arranged. The mob yelled for them to play 'God Save the King', and non-compliance with the request seemed to exasperate them beyond all bounds. At about twenty minutes past eleven o'clock they endeavoured to turn out the lights in the Central Hall, but were not successful. The police drove the rowdies down to the Entrance Hall and ejected them by main force, many of the mob being bodily thrown out. It was just after midnight, however, before the building was completely cleared of the rioters. (*The Freeman's Journal*, 17 November 1907)

An *Irish Times* report on the same incident is broadly similar, but describes a smaller crowd, less 'rowdyism', and a faster and more effective police response.

BUILDING IN PROGRESS

The official record of the Exhibition is somewhat reticent concerning the progress of construction. There are, however, other sources.

The Dublin Trades Council met with the Executive Committee of the International Exhibition at the end of October 1905. It was agreed that local labour would be employed in the construction period, that fair wages would be paid and that Irish materials would be used. The only disagreement arose over the Trades Council proposal that no overtime would be worked. 'Surely there could be no better way (of giving employment to the workers of Dublin) than by employing all workers that were out of employment, instead of working a limited number at high pressure,' noted Mr Mullen, a member of the council deputation. The Executive Committee thought it a 'novel thing', and refused to consider it.

The deputation was also reassured that there was no intention of importing one or more of the buildings from the Capetown Exhibition, as it would appear that the building concerned had been sold before the Irish Exhibition organisers could arrange its purchase. (*Irish Independent*, 31 October 1905)

By February 1906, the work had begun in earnest with upwards of 800 men on site. The Institute of Architects, however, harboured a grudge, and gave it full vent at their annual meeting in 1905:

There is one matter of public importance which occurred during the year, and in regard to which this report should not be silent, namely, the action of the committee of the Irish International Committee in going across the water for design and contractors for the buildings which they propose to erect at Ballsbridge … So much feeling has been aroused among the members of this Institute, owing to the extraordinary action of the promoters of the Exhibition, that it is difficult to deal with the matter. Suffice it to say, had the promoters approached this Institute, laid the whole matter before its council, explained (if such be the case) that the funds at the committee's disposal did not justify it in employing an architect; secured by competition or otherwise, under the ordinary recognised scale of professional remuneration, the council ventures to assert that, rather than be a party to the extraordinary method adopted for obtaining designs for an Irish International Exhibition, it would have gladly nominated a committee of its members – architects of repute in this city – who would have placed their services gratuitously in the hands of the Exhibition Committee. The fact has apparently been lost sight of, that the Exhibition of 1907 should, in its design, as well as in the exhibits it will contain, display the condition of Contemporary Architectural Art in Ireland. (*The Irish Builder and Engineer*, 10 February 1906)

Yesterday afternoon, by invitation of President and Council of the Irish International Exhibition, 1907, a large party of gentlemen attended at Herbert Park, Ballsbridge, where the Exhibition is to be held, and inspected the works and buildings now in course of construction. The gathering was thoroughly representative of the mercantile and professional classes of Dublin, while there was a good attendance of English and Continental visitors and journalists. (*The Irish Times*, 18 July 1906)

The visitors were well pleased with all they saw. The buildings have a very stately effect, and though, of course, of a purely temporary character, have much of the quality of stone structures. The general scheme is of a central hall, with radiating wings, and various independent halls. There is no doubt but that, at the present rate of progress, the buildings will be fully completed in good time for the opening ceremony, some ten months hence, Needless to say, the pretty surroundings of 'Pembroke Park', even encumbered as the site still is with the refuse and debris of buildings, add vastly to the general effect of the buildings, so that it can be imagined what a fine effect will be presented when the grounds are effectively laid out, with verdant lawns, gay flowers, sparkling fountains and well-kept walks.

...After luncheon ... Mr James Shanks, the chief executive officer, read an official statement, in the course of which he gave some interesting particulars of the extent of the buildings, and particulars relating to the Exhibition generally. Mr Shanks said that the buildings at the present stage, incomplete as they are, had been greatly admired, and there was general agreement that they would be worthy of Dublin, of the importance of the purpose which they are to serve, and credit to the committee, the consulting architects, and the contractors. It may interest the company, he added, to know something of the size of these buildings. The floor of the wing in which the luncheon was held was nearly 13,000 feet superficial. The area of the entire centre building, including the four wings, is almost 100,000 feet superficial, or nearly eight times the size of the hall. The area of the machinery pavilion will be 90,000 feet superficial, or nearly eight times the size of this hall. The Concert Hall and restaurant will each be about the size of this hall. The Fine Art

A bird's-eye sketch of the Herbert Park exhibition grounds.

Gallery will have an area of 30,000 feet superficial, and several other buildings rang-
ing from 15,000 to 50,000 feet superficial in area have yet to be erected.

The whole of the buildings have been designed by the contractors, Messrs
Humphreys, of London, Messrs Kaye, Parry and Ross acting as consulting architects.
(*The Irish Builder*)

By December 1906 the Executive Committee of the Exhibition was in a position
to report that space in the Grand Central Palace had been completely taken up, as
was three-quarters of the space in the Palace of Mechanical Arts, 'It is expected that
within a short time the letting over every foot of the available area will have been
completed and paid for.' (*Irish Independent*, 11 December 1906) The same report
noted that decisions on the sideshows had been made, to include 'a Water chute,
switchback railway, the rivers of Ireland, electric boats on the lake, and a hall of
mirrors'.

The Irish Builder visited the site at the end of April 1907:

When we visited the buildings last week we were surprised to find the work so back-
ward, although the main structures, with the exception of the French Pavilion, were
finished, the stalls were not at all completed, and but a few exhibits were visible or any
sign of them. Nevertheless, we were reliably informed all would be in readiness for the
4th, the date fixed for the opening ceremony.

The main entrance is from Ballsbridge. Access is given through a large detached
hall, with a raised way to cross a laneway which intervenes. This large hall is, we
understand, known as the Celtic Hall, and the most prominent position in its centre
is a remarkably finely modelled figure of 'Erin', by Messrs Worshing and Trautner, of
the Angle, Ranelagh, Dublin; sculptors and modellers. Very few other exhibits were
visible.

Regaining the open, the vista presents a very imposing aspect – the walks (still in an
unfinished condition) and the pleasant green sward and budding flowers and foliage,
with the beautiful background of the Dublin mountains, completing a very pretty
picture. Many artisans and labourers were at work on the buildings and grounds.

All the buildings are of corrugated iron; the main facades covered with fibrous
plaster. Internally they are all very plain, but many interesting and clever forms of
cheap and strong roofing construction and bracing are well worthy of study and
highly creditable to the contractors. Some extraordinary statements have for some
time past been current in the city as to the enormous outlay on the building structures comprising the Exhibition, but these rumours may safely be dismissed as gross
exaggerations, as the buildings are all of plain and simple construction, and we
have no doubt, are being erected economically at modest cost. At the same time
we cannot help regretting, once again, that the architectural design was not left
in the hands of an architect and an engineer, as originally settled, as the buildings,
although highly creditable from a constructional and economical point of view,

> leave much to be desired from an aesthetic standpoint, and betray the want of the architect's guiding hand in the details, and the want of breadth and unity of conceptions. It is one of those matters in which the foreigner shine. The main entrance from Ballsbridge, for instance, is utterly unworthy of its position as the chief entry into a great Irish Exhibition in the metropolis of Dublin. Needless to say, had the matter of design been left in the hands of the original distinguished architect, or had the committee appointed his successor as responsible architect rather than as consultant, (who, of course, cannot be blamed for what has occurred), something far different would have been presented to the citizens, and the foreign visitors, as a first impression of the great International Exhibition.
>
> With the lawns in good order and the flowers in bloom, the grounds should present a most attractive appearance, especially at night, when illuminated by the myriads of electric fairy lamps outlining the buildings, as is part of the electrical scheme. The Exhibition buildings have been the subject of much exaggerated and fulsome praise upon the part of some of the Dublin daily journals, so exaggerated as to be ludicrous. One such declaration describes the buildings as a 'Dreamland of Fairy Palaces!' Such criticism serves no purpose.
>
> The conduct of the Exhibition management has been the subject of a good deal of adverse and almost continual criticism, but no useful purpose is now to be served by this either; the fair way to look on the matter is to wish the enterprise every possible success, financial and otherwise. One statement, however, which has been freely made, and constitutes a severe reflection on the Dublin building trade – namely, that the buildings could not have been put up by any Dublin contractor – remains to be refuted, now that the buildings are practically completed. That statement may now be pronounced as having been made without any foundation, and we can safely say the Exhibition buildings could have been promptly, satisfactorily and economically constructed by the Dublin building trade. (*The Irish Builder*, 4 May 1907)

On the night before the official opening, one of the men painting the ceiling of the Entrance Hall at the Ballsbridge entrance was killed when a piece of the scaffolding collapsed. Three men fell; scaffold-builder Anthony Nolan of 13 Great Longford Street, held onto a gas pipe and survived unscathed, another man was slightly injured, but Francis Mooney, aged thirty-one, of 19 Lower Dorset Street, suffered fatal head injuries after plunging twenty-eight feet to the ground.

The County Coroner, Christopher Friery, held the inquest at the City of Dublin Hospital, Baggot Street, on the day the Exhibition opened. 'It was rather a pity that what they all hoped would be a great Exhibition should have brought sadness to at least one home on the eve of the opening', he noted.

A verdict of accidental death was returned by the jury, adding a rider recommending the widow of the deceased to the consideration of his employer, Messrs Dockrell, South Great George's Street. (*Evening Telegraph*, Monday 6 May 1907)

Nearly two weeks after the official opening, finishing work was still ongoing:

> The glorious weather yesterday was particularly favourable to a place like the Irish International Exhibition, and it was surprising that there was not a record crowd. Still the grounds and buildings were well filled during the afternoon and evening. The Canadian Pavilion was crowded. It is the chief indoor attraction, being brilliantly lighted, and containing a great variety of exhibits cleverly arranged. Things were quieter in the Machinery Hall and the Hall of Industry. Many workmen were still busy at late hour last night around the Water chute, and the operations at the island on the lake aroused much curiosity. There was nothing beyond the stands in the Central Hall at night, and this, which was formerly the favourite resort, seems, in the absence of special attractions, to have lost much of its drawing power. (*Evening Telegraph*, 15 May 1907)

As late as August, a letter appeared in the *Irish Independent* (9 August 1907) which shows that weatherproofing was still not top of the agenda:

> May I suggest to the Exhibition Executive the necessity for laying gravel on the main walk from the Entrance Hall to the Grand Central Palace? It was pitiful to-day when the rain came down so heavily about four o'clock to see lightly shod lady visitors being obliged to walk in thick mud when leaving the buildings. (English visitor)

PACKING THEM IN

From the earliest part of the Exhibition it was recognised by the organisers that it was imperative to maximise the numbers attending from around Ireland, as well as from overseas. Matters were not left to chance; large employers were particularly targeted, as were entire towns and villages. The following reports, all from the *Irish Independent*, give some idea of the numbers involved.

> 5 September: In Banagher the day was recognised as a general holiday, and everybody who could at all manage it in the locality took advantage of the greatly reduced fares offered by the Great Southern and Western Railway Company.
>
> The Great Northern Railway Company had also a busy day. Special fares from Belfast attracted an immense crowd, and there were also excursions from Warrenpoint and Dundalk.
>
> 11 September: A popular excursion has been arranged by the Galway Mechanics' Institute to take place from the Citie of the Tribes on Tuesday, 17th inst. It is expected that the local merchants will give their employees an opportunity of availing of the trip.

A special train with excursionists for the Exhibition will leave Kilmallock to take up passengers by request of the people of that locality. The day will be observed in Kilmallock as a general holiday.

13 September: The crowded condition of the streets during the past few weeks shows that our country cousins were waiting for the opportunity to visit Dublin this year. Soon after the Exhibition was opened we called the attention of the Irish railway companies to the rich harvest which was assured them if only they had the enterprise to avail of it. Hundreds of thousands of country people were but awaiting the reasonable inducements of fast excursion trains and cheap fares to the capital. The railway companies, as a whole, were rather slow in taking action, but now that they have moved, the results, as we anticipated, are proving eminently satisfactory to the carrying companies and to the public. Practically every excursion train that has been run into Dublin recently has been crowded to its utmost capacity, and the cheaper the fares the greater the number of travellers. Now that harvest work is to a great extent over, the numbers of country folk free to take their holidays will be daily increasing, and granted a continuance of the present fine weather, the railway excursions should prove profitable up to the closing days of the Exhibition.

14 September: The Duke of Edinburgh has made arrangement to send his staff of employees at Lismore, numbering 150, to the Exhibition … giving free tickets and paying the expenses of each employee. It is expected that some 500 excursionists will travel by the special train.

Ballina Urban Council has decided to make Wednesday, 25th inst., a general holiday in the town, in order to afford the people an opportunity of visiting the Exhibition.

Elaborate arrangements are being made in Ballinrobe to secure the success of the excursion from that town to Dublin on Tuesday next. All the local traders have promised to close their establishments on the day named.

19 September: The Great Western Railway of England are announcing another excursion from South Wales to Dublin for Sunday night, the 23rd inst. The two trains run by the same company on 6 and 13 September carried over 740 and 650 passengers respectively.

25 September: The Irish International Exhibition has been a good thing for the Irish railway companies, as well as, naturally, for the Dublin United Tramways Co. No doubt it has given an enormous fillip to business in many directions, the extent of which cannot readily be ascertained, but in the case of the companies mentioned we have the traffic returns in verification of the fact.

The following shows the increases in the traffic receipts of the principal Irish railway lines and of the Dublin Tramways Co., from the beginning of the year to the week ending 20 September:

	Total up to 1 July	Total for year up to 20 September
G.S. and W.R	£17,670	£38,193
G.N.R.	£14,329	£30,889
M.G.W.R.	£9,887	£17,152
D.U.T.	£9,055	£29,393

In the case of the G.S. and W.R. there is, of course, another contributory element to the increase, viz. the Rosslare line, and in the case of the Tramways Co. we have to make an allowance for the taking over of the Howth section.

2 October: The excursions for the day were from the following places: Arklow, Ballybrophy, Gorey, Borris-in-Ossory, Inch, Donaghmore, Lisduff, Johnstown, Mountrath, Rathdowney, Errill, Galmoy, Crosspatrick, Patrickswell. A second excursion has been arranged from Lismore for Monday next, and it will also bring contingents from Fermoy and Mallow.

8 October: From Limerick some 1,400 travelled and from Queenstown 700. Tomorrow Kells will be closed up while its people visit the Exhibition.

18 October: A most interesting episode in the history of the Exhibition took place yesterday, when a very large party of the boys of the Industrial School, Artane, paid a visit to the Ballsbridge Palace of Industrial Exhibits. The boys, headed by their magnificent brass and reed band, marched nearly 700 strong from the institution at Artane, through the city – accompanied by some 20 of the Christian Brothers and several assistant teachers ... Arrangements were made with the Exhibition authorities by which the boys were enabled to visit all the sideshows as well as the main features of the Exhibition, and they were eagerly availed of ... between four and five o'clock the boys were taken back as far on the way home as the Crescent, Fairview, by electric tram, tens of the Tram Co.'s cars being requisitioned for the purposes of the trip.

FAIRS OF THE FUTURE

As the International Exhibition entered its final weeks there was added interest in a report from the Board of Trade Committee on the advisability of Great Britain joining in a future International Exhibition. Issued in early October, it concluded that progress in advertising had reduced the importance of such events. It also regretted that the exhibitions had often less to do with industry than with popular amusement. Those reservations apart, the report noted the importance of attendance at some exhibitions and called for continuity of organisation from exhibition to exhibition.

The *Irish Times* wrote:

The coincidence of the Irish International Exhibition makes the report of the Board of Trade's Committee on the whole question of which exhibitions a particularly interesting one for Irish readers. Of late years more than one British manufacturer has come to be somewhat doubtful about the practical value of these great accumulations of industrial and commercial achievement. The expense of taking part in them is a very serious and definite item on the accounts. His ultimate profit is far less readily ascertained, and, like the proverbial bread upon the waters, may come back to him only after many days. We are glad to think that the manufacturer's doubts are likely to be partially, if not altogether, dispersed by the verdict of the Board of Trade's body of experts. The committee is, 'on the whole, disposed to think' that, even though immediate results may sometimes be disappointing, the systematical representation of a nation's industries at great International Exhibitions cannot fail to be ultimately of material advantage to the commercial development of that country ... So strongly is the committee convinced of this necessity that it urges that British participation in all future exhibitions should be systemised under the direct auspices of the Government.

We find even less point in the objection that the main purpose of recent exhibitions has been 'to attract visitors' and not to promote trade interests. It seems to us that the promotion of trade interests at an exhibition depends very largely on the number of people who are attracted to it, and that every legitimate means of increasing the flow at the turnstiles ought to be welcomed by every sensible exhibitor. The report mentions, however, one complaint with which we confess that we have a good deal of sympathy:

'Another consideration which appears to weigh with manufacturers of standing is the unbusiness-like and undignified manner in which they are apt to be mixed up with that they call "fakers" – i.e. the paltry dealers in cheap articles of ornament and amusement, which do not represent British industry.'

It is unquestionable that the 'faker' element in recent exhibitions has detracted very considerably not merely from their dignity and importance as national undertakings, but from their financial value to the traders of the centres where they are held. We are sorry to know that this has been the case, to some extent, at the present Exhibition in Dublin. It may be very difficult for the Exhibition authorities to prevent the intrusion of the 'faker', but there can be no doubt that this intrusion is a distinct injunction to the exhibitors and to local business interests. Traders who guarantee the expenses of an exhibition in the legitimate hope that it will react favourably on their own trade have good reason to complain when they find that their enterprise has only resulted in the influx of an undesirable class of business competitors. (9 October 1907)

GOING, GOING...

As the Exhibition drew to a close there was much speculation about whether or not it could continue in 1908. Some details became public at a meeting of Pembroke Council when a letter from the Exhibition solicitors was read out:

Dear Sir,

The Executive of the Exhibition have become aware of a very widespread feeling in favour of maintaining the structures in Herbert Park, and repeating next summer an exhibition of a somewhat similar character to the present one.

Those who are responsible for the existing undertaking sympathise with this desire, and are anxious to do anything in their power to give effect to it, as they believe it would meet with a large measure of success.

This project can only, however, be carried out if the Pembroke Council are willing to extend the term for the use of Herbert Park.

The Present (Incorporated) Company, who are the lessees of the Park are not themselves, owing to their relations with the guarantors, but if the Pembroke Council are consenting parties, a responsible syndicate would be willing to purchase all the Company's assets, with a view to repeating the Exhibition next year.

We are directed, therefore, to ask your council if they approve of the suggestion contained in this letter, that they would be good enough to extend the lease of the Park for one year on the same terms and conditions as those on which it is now held.

...As the buildings must be sold for removal on the close of the Exhibition, unless the proposed arrangement goes through meantime, and as nothing definite can be done except in agreement with your council, you will, we are sure, appreciate the importance of an early decision on the subject.

Yours faithfully,
Casey and Clay
(15 October)

Pembroke Urban Council last evening discussed a letter which they had received from Messrs Casey and Clay, solicitors to the Irish International Exhibition (Incorporated) Company, asking the council to extend the lease of Herbert Park for one year, viz. to 30 June 1909, on the same terms and conditions as those on which it is now held, with a view of maintaining the structures in the Park, and repeating next summer, an exhibition of a somewhat similar character to the present one, a responsible syndicate being willing to purchase all the company's assets.

The council ultimately, on the motion of Mr Ramsey, seconded by Mr Cahill, referred the matter to a committee of the whole house.

Mr Ramsey said he was strongly in favour of what the syndicate proposed to do. At the same time he would like to have more information in regard to it, and that there should be a special meeting of the council then called to consider the question.

…Mr Hewat [said] the Exhibition was overrun with sideshows which were not at all pleasing to the residents of the township, and unless he was assured that some important changes for the better were made by the syndicate he would be entirely opposed to having the Exhibition there for any longer time.

The chairman (Mr W. Beckett) said that he did not see how the ratepayers would benefit by the continuing of the Exhibition, which had not proved beneficial to the township or the city. Some of the sideshows were popular enough and not objectionable, but others, especially the machine music, were an injury to the township.

Mr Cahill considered that the holding of the Exhibition for another season would be of very great benefit to the township. No less than £100,000 had been paid in wages to Dublin Artisans arising out of the holding of the Exhibition, and he considered that a great advantage.

The syndicate, he understood, was composed of very responsible people. When the Exhibition closed there would be a very big deficit. The syndicate, he thought, should be afforded an opportunity of wiping out that deficit, and giving a good name to Dublin, by showing that its citizens were able to make a financial success of such a great venture. As to the sideshows, he never heard any complaints made, but everything was conducted in the best possible manner. (*Irish Independent*, 15 October 1907)

The application which has been made to the Pembroke Urban District Council to extend the lease of Herbert Park for another year raised a point of considerable importance to the people of Dublin, and indeed of all Ireland. The extension of the lease is required to enable a syndicate to take over the Exhibition buildings as they stand, and re-open them next year … There must, however, be still many people in the country who have not yet had a convenient opportunity of visiting the Exhibition, and who would most probably avail of a second chance of doing so. Again, the Dublin people have come to regard the picturesque grounds, and handsome buildings of the Exhibition with their many attractions somewhat in the light of institutions, and are already induced to wonder what they should do next year without them. To all these, as well as to the many business people in Dublin, who have profited by the great influx of visitors caused by the Exhibition, the news that it is proposed to re-open it next year will be received with satisfaction. (*Irish Independent*, 16 October)

The same issue carried a letter from 'Season Ticket No. 2' arguing the case in favour of continuing the Exhibition:

A petition of ratepayers should be presented to the Earl of Pembroke, asking him to allow some of the beautiful buildings in Herbert Park, to stand for another year. I am sure that, when presenting this fine park to the township, Lord Pembroke had in view the greater good of the greater number, and not only the likes or dislikes of a few inhabitants of Elgin and Clyde roads, who will never visit the Park at all.

The Committee of the Pembroke Council met on 17 October and agreed, subject to the approval of Lord Pembroke, to grant the Exhibition a nine-month extension to late 1908.

On the same day the Port and Docks Board discussed a letter from James Shanks, Chief Executive Officer of the Exhibition, 'It is believed that, owing to the unseasonable weather during the greater part of the summer, the Exhibition [in the summer and autumn months of 1908] would show quite as many visitors as the existing one.'

It was only a matter of time before somebody raised the spectre of Donnybrook Fair – Bindon B. Stoney, of 14 Elgin Road, rose to the occasion in a letter to the *Irish Times* on 21 October:

> The present Exhibition professed to be an exhibition of arts and manufactures, and the committee in the main carried out their work in a highly creditable manner, but latterly, and probably with the object of increasing receipts, there have been added a baby incubator, a merry-go-round, with steam orchestra, several sing-swungs [sic], a dancing hall, and a tight-rope dancer. If public interest in a stale exhibition flags, profits will dwindle, and thus there may arise temptation to have more cheap shows, gaffs, swing-swungs, merry-go-rounds, dancing platforms, saloons, and similar devices for catering for a certain class of taste, and raising the win for a syndicate which naturally does not boast of philanthropic motives as a guide to its actions.
>
> When Lord Pembroke entertained the idea of presenting a park for the adornment of the district and the recreation of its inhabitants, he could little have anticipated that his noble gift might be turned into a sort of glorified Donnybrook Fair that would inevitably depreciate his property, and be objectionable to many of his tenants.

John H. Edge, 16 Clyde Road, also put the case against any continuance in a letter printed in the *Irish Times* of 9 November:

> My house and the other villas are held under most stringent clauses preserving them as private residences, and Lord Pembroke is bound to me and his other tenants not to permit the amenities of our residences to be interfered with.
>
> I wrote last month to Mr Fane Vernon, Lord Pembroke's agent, calling his attention to the fact that an attempt was being made to convert the Exhibition into a quasi-permanent institution. He sent round circulars to the owners and occupiers of Lord Pembroke's property, who would be more immediately affected by the further continuance of the Exhibition. Mr Vernon got a practically unanimous vote from them against its continuance for another year.

…As far as I could form any opinion, and my prejudices were against the Exhibition ever being held where it was, every care was taken by its promoters and by the police that its shows should be carried on with the least possible inconvenience to the district. Notwithstanding this, the shows were, in my opinion, most unpleasant to us all near it. Its quasi-permanent continuance would, in my opinion, be entirely inconsistent with the nature of the district, and ruinous to the value of the property in it.

The Pembroke Council meeting of 11 November, which narrowly passed a motion in favour of the Exhibition continuing, finally heard the views of Lord Pembroke, expressed in a letter from his agent, Fane Vernon, dated 25 October:

He considers that your council are honourably bound to him to lose as little time as possible in opening Herbert Park … Although the owners of the adjacent property have been willing to subordinate their own convenience to the good of the community, and consequently have made but few complaints as to the injury to the amenities of their property, caused by the inevitable noise and nuisance of the recent Exhibition, they have made it known that they are strongly opposed to any repetition of it, and have called on Lord Pembroke to protect their interests.

…Of course it might have been urged that Lord Pembroke has the power of a veto. This is no doubt true, but what his lordship desires is that both your council and he should work in harmony for the common good.

A second letter, noting that the council continued to consider the 1908 proposal, was brief and, in the use of the word 'provisional', carried a strong warning:

In order that there may be no misunderstanding about the matter, I now write to state definitely that his lordship cannot consent to your council's allowing the present Exhibition to be continued after to-day [9 November], the day on which it has been advertised to be closed, or their making any arrangements for another exhibition to be held in 1908.

I am further to say that his lordship looks to your council to now fulfil the conditions which were agreed upon at the time when he made the provisional gift of the ground.

The members of the council were, in the main, unimpressed by the implied threat; more than one stated that they should be in control of their own affairs and it was also noted that only half of the Exhibition grounds formed the gift from Lord Pembroke.

The meeting also observed that, of the voting cards that had been distributed by the Exhibition organisers to registered electors in the district, 1,582 were in favour of the Exhibition continuing, with just 69 against. Mr Beckett objected to the votes as they contained only an option in favour of the proposals, those who voted against had to write their objection on the cards. In his belief the vote was tainted, 'It was fair to assume that those who did not vote in favour of the re-opening were against it. 1,582 replies had been sent in, which was only about one-fourth of the rated occupiers of the township.'

The following day an *Irish Independent* editorial took the view that Lord Pembroke would continue his opposition, 'We are loath to believe that Lord Pembroke will oppose the freely expressed opinions of the ratepayers of the township and the Urban Council, and persist in vetoing their decision.'

Crucially, however, the council members, while willing to verbally express their independence from Lord Pembroke had, in the resolution passed, left the final decision to him:

> That the council consent to extend the lease to the International Exhibition for seven months from the expiration of the present lease on 1 July 1908, at an increased rent, at the rate of 1,500 for such extension, subject to the following conditions: that consent of Lord Pembroke be obtained...

A letter from Fane Vernon on 20 November effectively brought the matter to a close:

> I had already been favoured by the Clerk of the Pembroke Urban District Council with a copy of the resolution passed by his Board at their recent meeting, and I duly communicated the same to Lord Pembroke, who has since written personally to the council, stating that he will under no circumstances consent to the further use of Herbert Park for the purpose indicated.
>
> Under these circumstances I do not think that I need trouble the Exhibition Committee to enter into any explanation on the subject.

On the same day the *Irish Independent* published the details of the annual meeting of Messrs Hely's Ltd, reporting a slight drop in profits:

> Mr Charles Wisdom Hely, Managing Director, said that gross profits last year had been £8,724. This year they had dropped to £8,099. But that difference might easily be accounted for by an exceptional circumstance in the history of the firm's working.
>
> At their last annual meeting the question of supporting the Irish International Exhibition came up, and they had decided to do so, as they recognised that the Exhibition would tend to the country's advancement, and enable the firm to secure a foothold in their commercial transactions which would be of the greatest use to them in the future. The directors had paid £4,000 for the rights they obtained at the Exhibition, without, at the time, having any opportunity of making any very large profit. But they felt that they would be fully justified, for the future of the concern, in acting as they did in the matter.

He might add, that while the £4,000 that they had expended upon the Irish International Exhibition had been recouped them, nevertheless the responsibilities in connection with the organisation of their stands there had been very great.

James Shanks, the former Chief Executive Officer of the Exhibition, wrote an open letter to the Exhibition guarantors on 25 November:

As already intimated in the Press, my official connection with the Irish International Exhibition, extending over a period of three and a half years, terminated at the closing of the Exhibition on 9th inst. If my relation with the enterprise had been no more than official, my interest in it would have ceased naturally and properly on the same date; but, as more than half the Guarantee Fund was obtained by my successful work amongst a wide personal connection, I still owe a duty to those who subscribed at my request. In discharge of that duty, I have to point out certain circumstances which tend to increase the liability of guarantors, and suggest for the consideration a method of lessening the risk.

The present indebtedness to the Bank of Ireland is, roughly, £100,000, and interest thereon is accumulating at the rate of more than £500 a month.

The conditions of the guarantee do not impose any obligation on the Bank to enforce payment of a call upon all guarantors, and the Bank may demand from such guarantors as it may select the payment up to the full amount of their guarantees of any deficiency in the result of a general call.

Although the Exhibition has been closed for more than a fortnight, I am unaware of any intention on the part of the committee in charge of the property of a desire to take the guarantors into their confidence, or consult with them about winding-up arrangements.

The steps necessary to secure such a prompt and advantageous realisation of the buildings and other valuable assets as would minimise the liability of guarantors have been delayed. The delay is attributed to the existence of a hope or expectation that a projected syndicate will be able to make arrangement for a second year of the Exhibition, and the purchase of the assets for a lump sum. Meantime, many inquiries about buildings which might have led to their profitable sale, have not been seriously considered, and if there is further delay of the kind a forced sale at ruinous prices may become inevitable at a later date, if, as is probable, syndicate prospects do not mature successfully.

…guarantors generally would do well to consider the propriety of appointing a small representative committee of their own number to watch their interests, to act on their behalf in harmony with the bank, and to co-operate on a basis to be mutually agreed upon with the Exhibition Committee.

To such a committee of guarantors, I should, if requested, be glad to render any assistance in my power, without fee, but my participation is not an essential consideration.

In fact the Exhibition organisers were already taking steps to liquidate their assets. Advertisements for the auction of fixtures and fittings started appearing in December, and the sale of the buildings was advertised in early 1908.

Pembroke Urban District Council decided to stick to the letter of their contract with the Exhibition and, on 29 June, insisted that the contractors, engaged in restoring the site to its original condition, should leave, even though work was not complete. A request that an additional two to three weeks be granted to complete restoration of Herbert Park was rejected.

Shortly afterwards the council went to court, claiming damages of over £10,000 from the Exhibition guarantors. On Friday 23 April 1909 the case was finally decided by a jury (which had visited the site), and the council received damages of just £500, with both sides ordered to pay their costs.

With the Pembroke case concluded, the way was clear for the final meeting of creditors to take place. That meeting was held on 4 June and the Exhibition was finally laid to rest.

Herbert Park opened as a public park on 19 August 1911. The lake is all that remains of the Irish International Exhibition of 1907.

Due to space constraints, it was impossible to include all of the information that I have accumulated on the Irish International Exhibition of 1907. If you are interested in hearing about my research, please feel free to email me at kenfinlay@gmail.com

Record of the Irish International Exhibition 1907

ORIGIN OF THE PROJECT

The Irish International Exhibition of 1907 was, in large measure, a product of the movement for the revival of national industries, which had previously brought into existence the Cork International Exhibition of 1902-3. This latter display was one which reflected infinite credit on its organisers, but its extent was naturally limited by the amount of monetary resources at the disposal of its promoters. The total capital available – provided by voluntary cash contributions – was something under £30,000. Even with this small capital a creditable exhibition was organised.

In the early weeks of 1903, a series of articles were published in the Dublin *Irish Daily Independent*, from the pen of its editor, Mr W.F. Dennehy, pointing out the desirability of making attempts to co-ordinate and place on a practical basis the various isolated bodies which were working independently in different parts of the country for the attainment of a common purpose. The proposals put forward embraced two purposes. One of these was the establishment of a National Institute of Commerce and Industries, and the other the holding of an Irish International Exhibition on a large and thoroughly comprehensive scale in Dublin at an early date.

The articles published in the *Irish Daily Independent* attracted a great deal of attention, and evoked expressions of approval from Irishmen of all creeds and parties. The Earl of Belmore, the late Lord Viscount Powerscourt, Lord Castletown of Upper Ossory, and many other persons of influence in national concerns, wrote letters expressing sympathy with the policy advocated and their desire to assist in securing the largest results from the 'industrial awakening' which was taking place all over the land. In face of the widespread manifestations of desire that some definite action should be taken, a circular was issued by Lord Castletown and Mr W.F.

Dennehy, convening a semi-public meeting, to be held in the Shelbourne Hotel, on 4 February 1903, to consider the advisability of taking steps to hold, at an early date, an Industrial Conference, constituted on entirely non-sectarian and non-political lines. The response to this invitation was encouraging, with sympathetic messages being received from all parts of Ireland. The purpose of the meeting was known to have the approval of His Excellency the Earl of Dudley, Lord Lieutenant of Ireland.

The first resolution, proposed by Mr William Field, MP, and seconded by Mr Beattie, was as follows:

> That, in the opinion of this Meeting, it is eminently desirable to convene a completely representative Irish Industrial Conference, to be held in Dublin at an early date, with a view to the adoption of measures likely to result in the development of commerce and manufactures, and directed towards checking the constant stream of emigration from our shores.

The resolution, which was supported by the Right Hon. the Lord Mayor of Cork, Sir Edward Fitzgerald, Bart, Mr A. Gore Ryder, Mr E. Cunningham, Mr P.J. Lawlor, and Mr Edward Lee, JP, was unanimously adopted.

The second resolution, proposed by the Right Hon. the Recorder of Dublin, Sir Frederick Falkiner, and seconded by Mr P. J. O'Neill, JP, chairman Dublin County Council, was in the following words:

> That in order to give effect to the resolution which has been adopted, all those attending the present Meeting, or who have expressed approval of its objects, be appointed members of a committee – with power to add to their number – with a view to making the necessary arrangements for holding an Irish Industrial Conference.

This resolution also was unanimously adopted. A subscription list having been opened and a considerable amount subscribed, the High Sheriff was moved to the second chair, the proceedings terminating with votes of thanks to Lord Castletown and Mr Dennehy.

The first meeting of the committee appointed to organise an Industrial Conference was held in Jurys Hotel on Monday 9 February 1903.

On the motion of Mr C.L. Falkiner, seconded by Mr W. Graham, JP, it was unanimously resolved: 'That an Executive Committee be appointed, composed of the Honorable Treasurers and Honorary Secretaries, with Sir John Nutting, Bart, DL; Colonel Courtenay, CB, DL; Mr C. Litton Falkiner, BL; Mr Andre Beattie; Mr Vere Ward Brown; Mr Thomas Baker; Mr E.L. Richardson, and Mr John Gibbons.'

The Executive Committee thus appointed at once proceeded energetically with the work entrusted to it, meeting on 10, 13, 16, 18 and 24 February; 2, 9, 16, 23 and

30 March; 1, 7, 9 and 13 April. The result of its labours was the satisfactory organisation of the great Irish Industrial Conference.

The Conference assembled in the Great Hall of the Royal University, Earlsfort Terrace, on Wednesday 15 April 1903. The building was crowded by an influential and representative assembly. It is simply asserting the truth to say that certainly not within living memory had a gathering so completely combining all sections of the community in the prosecution of a common end been witnessed in Dublin or any other part of Ireland.

After the dispersal of the Irish Industrial Conference, following its appointment of two committees charged respectively with the duty of organising an Institute of Commerce and Industry, and establishing an International Exhibition, the Executive Committee, having fulfilled the purpose for which it was constituted, held two more meetings, on 16 and 20 April, for the purpose of winding-up its affairs and transferring the funds in its hands to the credit of its successors. It may safely be asserted that no better work or one more satisfactorily concluded was ever done for Ireland than that accomplished by the Executive Committee during its two months' existence.

The chairman [Right Hon. W.J. Pirrie, DL], on rising to address the meeting, was received with enthusiastic applause. Mr Pirrie began by congratulating the promoters of the Conference on the character of the gathering which they had assembled. It had drawn together men of different politics, different religions, different social standings, to do what they could to better the condition of their country. There was a momentous move before them that day. They had a golden opportunity to do great good if they only rose to the occasion.

On behalf of the North of Ireland he thanked the representatives of the other parts of Ireland for placing him – a representative of the industry of Belfast – in the chair. That was a business meeting. They had to decide if they were going to do something, to rely on their own exertions, and not place too much reliance on Government help. He was rather opposed to Government assistance when they could do so much for themselves. He was authorised by Mr Wyndham to say that he endorsed the remarks which he (Mr Pirrie) was making to them that day.

The Conference should realise that they should initiate a movement depending mainly on their own effort. Lord Iveagh and himself had felt obliged to show their countrymen and their neighbours that they could invest money in their own country with safety, with confidence and with the prospect of return. He instanced the experience of his own firm as a proof of how that confidence had been repaid. They must not be afraid of competition. They must work on serious lines. They must not look for the mere sympathy of outsiders. They must not appeal for it. Let them produce the very best article and at a price which would compete with the foreigner. Let them buy the cheapest commodity in the way of raw material they could obtain for the purposes of the manufacturing industries they would establish, and they would then be in a position to put the labour of their hands into them with the prospect of return.

The chairman's remarks on the subject of railway rates were followed with eager interest, and his statement of the results which he hoped to secure from the scheme of Lord Iveagh and himself was warmly applauded. As for the Exhibition project, Mr Pirrie expressed his pleasure that the date of the holding of it had been left open. If they waited for a time they might be able to hold an exhibition of their own industries.

It was useless to talk of the causes of the decay of industries. Let them get to work. Let them labour to stop the tide of immigration. Let them labour to keep at home the men who, in other lands, were the very cream of the industrial organisation which was creating competition with themselves. With a renewed plea for a policy of self-reliance, the chairman closed a practical, yet eloquent and impressive speech, amid the sympathetic cheers of the assembly.

The Lord Mayor of Dublin, the Right Hon. T.C. Harrington, BL, MP, proposed the first resolution. He said that the interest of the people outside in their proceedings was contingent on the promise they gave of doing something practical to revive Irish industries that would not be entirely dependent on appeals to sympathy. The time was propitious for such a movement. The Institute of Industry, which it was suggested to form, was of a kind that would combine the producer, the distributor, and the purchaser in a consultative union, to guard the interests of the whole country. If they forgot differences and were animated by a desire to select the best men on the Executive, who would work for the objects of the Institute, they could do great good. The explanation of a great deal of our loss of industry was to be found in the terrible decay of population within the past half century. If the controversies of the past, which centred on the land question, were once stilled, they could work with greater confidence for the industrial regeneration of Ireland.

The Lord Mayor of Cork put the issues before the meeting bluntly. They'd had enough of speaking, said his Lordship. They must now take off their coats and set to work. Let them support their own manufacturers. It was in the power of each of them to help. Was it not possible, for example, for an Irish manufacturer to make an Irish boot suitable for Irish feet? If the Government was to take up this industrial revival it would be a failure. The people themselves must do it. Let them help each other, and if they had a pound to spend let them spend it on articles of Irish manufacture.

The Earl of Belmore said that it was absolutely essential that the rising generation should have the benefit of the advice and direction which the proposed Institute would give.

Lord Castletown expressed the indebtedness of the Conference to Mr Dennehy for bringing them together, and he asked them to remember the deep debt of gratitude due to Mr Pirrie for his coming there that day.

The idea they had in their minds was that Ireland was not moving as fast as other countries. They had one of the greatest captains of industry in the chair. They had successful men present from other parts. They now wanted to fill up the gaps in other parts of the country. The young people had not the commercial or industrial training which they needed. Few people were better fitted intellectually for the fight than their own, but they knew not what to do. They wanted light and guidance, and that was what the Institute would provide. They wanted to help and supplement the work so well done by Mr Horace Plunkett and his coadjutors.

This was the first time that Irishmen from all parts of the country had met to organise, to educate, to co-operate, and to fight for supremacy in the industrial arena. Emigrants went to America to get work. There they had to work hard. Why not work at home? They wanted to create a centre of industrial thought, to which the people would naturally look for direction. That was the object of the Institute. They wanted to round off the corners which sometimes created friction between capital and labour. That was a business question, and more, it was the problem of the existence of their race. The men who created many small industries here and there were as useful as the millionaire. They were told that the Irishman was a fine fighter. Let him now stand on his own feet and fight for the industrial freedom of his country.

Count Moore said there was a belief that behind ministers and their sympathetic utterances was a more august influence, which was being exerted in the direction of helping forward the best interests of the country. There was a great opportunity for well-doing in this matter. If they wanted to keep the people at home they must better their circumstances. They could not expect them to live contentedly in the slums of the cities. They must have the habits and the means to improve themselves. They must better the conditions of the labouring classes, so that they can produce better work. Give them the chance of living decent, Christian lives, and it would repay the community a hundred-fold. None had a greater interest in the welfare of the worker than the captain of industry himself.

Sir James Murphy; Mr William Field, MP; Mr Alexander Shaw; Mr E.L. Richardson, and the Revd Denham Osborne, having addressed the meeting, Mr William M. Murphy was called on by the chairman to support the resolution. Mr Murphy, in the course of his remarks, said that:

> If speeches could regenerate Ireland, he thought she would be one of the most prosperous countries in the world. (Laughter) He, for one, thought that the man who did was a much more valuable man than the man who spoke ('hear, hear' and applause). The want of such an Institute was generally admitted, and the fact that there was room for it would also be admitted by everybody who had fully considered the subject ('hear, hear'). He had no doubt there was room for it without treading on the heels or toes of any other existing organisation ('hear, hear'). As one of those who had been engaged in organising this movement, he would like to disclaim any desire

Park Gate, Dublin.

Phoenix Park was the original site considered for the exhibition.

whatever to interfere in the least degree with any existing organisation ('hear, hear'). Their desire, on the contrary, was to cordially work with them, and also to co-operate with any other organisation that may be formed hereafter for similar purposes.

The possibility of Ireland providing not only themselves, but others in other parts of the world, with industrial products, was, he thought, sufficiently proved by the fact that in a number of cases they had industries in Ireland which were holding their own against any industries in the world (applause). They had, for example, the shipbuilding, with which their chairman was connected (applause), and they had also a number of other industries in Ireland, which were subject to the disadvantages which are supposed to weigh against any industrial enterprise in this country. Still, these industries were, as he said, holding their own. They were in the habit of blaming everybody and everything except themselves. One time it was the railways and the railway rates, another time it is the fault of legislation, and always there was something; but want of enterprise and energy were never mentioned.

Well, he believed that want of enterprise and want of energy were at the bottom of the present position of Ireland ('hear, hear' and applause). Unfortunately it was the case that, as a rule, the Irishman did not think enough of himself. He did not value his own ability until he came alongside other men from other countries, and then he came to realise that he is a better man than he thought himself ('hear, hear'). The workingmen of Ireland were all right, but they required to be intelligently directed. He also thought that anyone starting an industry in this country must provide the very best and newest machinery. They must not expect to make a fortune in a hurry ('hear, hear'). Some men whom he knew had failed in business because they had not the patience to bear losses in the beginning ('hear, hear'). Others, who had succeeded, did so because they persevered against, and triumphed over, the obstacles which met them at the start. Irishmen had plenty of dash, but, unfortunately, they lacked perseverance very often ('hear, hear'). He cordially supported the resolution, and he was sure the names submitted to the meeting would be found quite willing and competent to successfully carry out the objects of the Conference (applause).

The Meeting then took up the consideration of the question of an International Exhibition, and the Earl of Mayo, in an eloquent speech, proposed the following resolution, 'That in the opinion of this Conference it is desirable to give effect to the widespread wish to hold an International Exhibition in Dublin.' That motion was unanimously passed as was a second, 'That a committee, consisting of the following noblemen and gentlemen, be appointed to take the necessary steps to carry out the previous resolution, and to make a request to His Majesty's Government for a suitable site for the intended Exhibition in the Phoenix Park.'

PRELIMINARY ORGANISATION

On Wednesday 22 April 1903, the first meeting was held in the Mansion House of the two committees appointed at the Irish Industrial Conference, for the purpose of organising an Institute of Commerce and Industries, and an International Exhibition. As practically all those attending were members of both committees, it was decided to sit in common.

On the motion of Lord Belmore, seconded by Lord Castletown, the chair was taken by the Right Hon. T.C. Harrington, MP, Lord Mayor. The first practical steps taken were to appoint two subcommittees, one to prepare a scheme for the establishment of an Institute of Commerce and Industries, and the other to act similarly in the case of the proposed International Exhibition. To the first-named subcommittee were referred draft constitutions for an Institute, prepared by the Right Hon. Sir Frederick Falkiner, Recorder of Dublin; Sir John Nutting, Bart.; Mr Thomas Baker; Mr E.L. Richardson, and Mr Dennehy.

Having arranged for the holding of further meetings of the subcommittee, namely of the Institute Committee on Mondays, and of the Exhibition Committee on Wednesdays, both at 4 p.m., the meeting adjourned. So far as the scope of the present work is concerned, the further proceedings of the subcommittee appointed to organise an Institute of Commerce and Industries lie entirely outside it. Nevertheless, as a matter of historic knowledge, it may be recorded that the subcommittee did succeed in framing a scheme for the establishment of an Institute, and that this was embodied in the Memorandum and Articles of an Association, to be incorporated as one not carried on for purposes of personal profit. The Memorandum and Articles, having been examined by Counsel for the Board of Trade, were duly approved for

W.M. Murphy.

registration, but the committee decided to defer incorporation pending the holding of the International Exhibition, hoping that from its profits might be provided sufficient endowment to place the Institute on a basis of permanent national usefulness.

The first independent meeting of the special Exhibition Committee was held on Wednesday 29 April 1903. It was largely attended, the Lord Mayor presiding, and definite steps were taken to push the work in hand forward. It was unanimously agreed to recommend the General Committee to undertake the holding of an International Exhibition in Dublin at a date not later than 1906, the intervening period to be devoted to securing the necessary financial resources, to hold a public meeting for the purpose of organising a Guarantee Fund, as well as to request the Lord Mayor, MP, Lord Mayo, and Lord Castletown to interview the Chief Secretary, Mr George Wyndham, MP, in order to ascertain if the Government would give a site in the Phoenix Park for the buildings of the intended Exhibition, and financial support to the undertaking.

Eventually, at a meeting of the General Organising Committee of the Exhibition, appointed by Industrial Conference, held on Thursday 4 June 1903, thoroughly practical action was taken with a view to giving the movement tangible shape. The minutes of the committee record that it was proposed by Mr William M. Murphy, seconded by Mr John Mooney, and unanimously resolved:

> That a subcommittee be appointed to prepare an outline scheme for the proposed
> Irish International Exhibition (1906), dealing with the question of site, character of

buildings, general characteristics, probable cost, and means of financing the enterprise. That the following gentlemen constitute the subcommittee: Lt Col. Plews, Mr W.M. Murphy, Sir Thomas Drew, Mr George Ashlin, Mr William Anderson, Mr J.H. Ryan, Mr Cutler, Mr J. Shanks, Mr John Mooney, Mr Charles McCarthy, Mr Spencer Harty, Mr R.S. Tresilian, Alderman Cotton, Mr T.A. O'Farrell, Mr Charles Dawson, Mr J.R. O'Connell, and the Honorary Treasurers and Secretaries.

The gentlemen appointed by this resolution went vigorously about the work entrusted to them, with the result that on 29 June 1903 they were able to report to the Exhibition subcommittee the result of the extensive enquiries they had undertaken. Their report was as follows:

Since their appointment the members of the subcommittee have devoted a considerable amount of time to the examination of various sites which were suggested as suitable for the purpose in view. It will be recognised that until the actual location of the Exhibition has been definitely decided, it will be impossible to put forward any general design as to the position of the various buildings, to come to any conclusion as to their character, or to form even an approximate idea as to their cost.

Under these circumstances, the subcommittee have carefully examined three possible sites in the Phoenix Park. One of these lies on the north side of the main road running from Parkgate Street to the Phoenix Column, and extends from the Zoological Gardens to the entrance to the Viceregal Lodge, at the intersection of the crossroads leading to the column. This site would, of course, include the present Polo ground. The second site examined lies on the south side of the main road, extending from the present cricket enclosures for a considerable distance towards the Magazine Fort. The third site suggested, and which was also viewed, lies within the Park, overlooking the River Liffey, and facing the University Boat Club. If this site were selected it would be necessary to acquire land on both sides of the river, on the southern side of the road to Chapelizod. The land in question, although at one time portion of the Park, is not now in possession of the Government.

During the sittings of the subcommittee it was strongly urged by several members that if a site could be secured anywhere in the southern suburbs of the city, the financial success of the Exhibition would be much more likely than if one were obtained in the Park. As a result, several sites were examined, but of these only one is, in the opinion of the subcommittee, fully suitable. It is a considerable expanse of ground, picturesquely wooded, and with ample water supply, lying between the River Dodder, Clyde and Morehampton Roads.

The greater portion of this land is in possession of Lord Pembroke, who has already promised it to the Pembroke District Council for the purpose of forming a public park. In an interview, however, which Mr Fane Vernon, DL, agent for the Pembroke Estate, accorded some of the members of the committee, that gentleman stated that if the District Council could be induced to waive their claim to occupation of the land

Main Road, Phoenix Park.

during the period of erection and holding of the Exhibition, he felt satisfied that Lord
Pembroke would give most favourable consideration to any request addressed to him
by the Exhibition Committee.

The chair, during the meeting at which this report was unanimously approved, was
occupied by the Right Hon. the Lord Mayor, MP (Mr T.C. Harrington), and the
committee decided to enter into immediate negotiations with the Pembroke Urban
District Council, with a view to obtaining a site for the intended Exhibition on the
lands in the possession of that body at Herbert Park.

On Thursday 28 July 1903, another meeting of the Exhibition subcommittee was
held in Jurys Hotel, College Green, to receive certain members of the Pembroke
Council, in the hope of arriving at a basis of agreement regarding the acquisition of
the Herbert Park lands.

This meeting marked an important stage in the history of the Exhibition.
Sir Robert Gardner frankly declared that he and his colleagues would be willing to facilitate the purposes of the committee if and when they had assurance
that its financial resources were adequate to the end in view. He further intimated that as the Pembroke Council was bound to construct two roads on the
lands required by the committee, one to cost £2,500, and the other £1,000,
he thought the amount to be paid by the committee, in the event of a ten-
ancy being arranged for, should be this sum of £3,500. Discussion followed,
and eventually, the representatives of the council having withdrawn, it was
unanimously agreed to request the Sites subcommittee to proceed as rapidly

as possible with the preparation of an outline scheme for the utilisation of the Herbert Park grounds.

In accordance with this injunction, the Sites subcommittee met on 31 July. At this meeting Mr George Ashlin, FRIBA, FRIAI, RHA, and Mr John H. Ryan, MA, M.Inst.CE, kindly consented, at the request of the committee, to prepare a rough plan of buildings and approximate estimate of the cost of utilising, for Exhibition purposes, the Herbert Park land, and two further plots, bounded respectively by Morehampton Road and Doctor's Walk, and Morehampton Road and the River Dodder. This latter land it was hoped to utilise as a stadium or sports ground, but eventually it was found impossible to acquire it on anything close to reasonable terms. Though the very attractive sketch plans prepared by Messrs Ashlin and Ryan were not ultimately carried out, it would be ungrateful not to acknowledge the valuable services rendered by the eminent architect and his engineer colleague. The plan devised by them, and the report accompanying – published as they were in the Press – more than anything else brought home to the public mind realisation of the feasibility of the work the committee had in hand.

On 7 December 1903, a meeting of the General Committee was held, under the presidency of the Hon. Mr Justice Boyd. At this a report from the Sites subcommittee was submitted, transmitting that prepared by Mr Ashlin and Mr Ryan. It was unanimously resolved, 'that the thanks of the Committee of the Irish International Exhibition, 1906, are heartily expressed to Mr George C. Ashlin and Mr J.H. Ryan, for the trouble and care taken by them in regard to the plans.'

It will be observed that at this time the date '1906' was still retained as part of the title of the Exhibition, there being, as yet, no reason to doubt that, as all along expected, Governmental aid on a generous scale would be forthcoming, so as to enable the opening of the Exhibition in that year.

A letter was read at this meeting from Mr J.C. Manly, Town Clerk of Pembroke District, stating that his council had decided to allow the committee the use of the ground in their possession at Clyde Road for three years, at an annual rent of £1,000, and the payment of all rates and taxes. It was resolved, 'That the terms proposed by the Pembroke Council be accepted, and the matter referred to the Special Site Committee to deal with, subject to a satisfactory agreement being submitted to and approved by the committee's solicitor.'

The principal site had now been secured, but additional land was needed, and four members of the committee, namely, Mr Vere Ward Brown, Mr Joseph Mooney, Mr John Mooney, and Mr Dennehy, were appointed to negotiate with the owners of these.

It will be observed that so far no definite steps had been taken towards the formation of the Guarantee Fund, the creation of which was essential to the holding of the Exhibition, and at this stage Mr W.M. Murphy, chairman of the Tramway Company, and a Director of the Great Southern and Western Railway Company, convened a meeting of the Chairmen of the Railways and Steamship Companies having their termini in Dublin, and, having pointed out the increase of traffic which might be expected from the holding of the Exhibition, obtained promises of substantial guarantees.

The subcommittee appointed to negotiate with the owners of the lands adjoining Herbert Park immediately entered into communication with the representatives of the latter, and were successful in acquiring more than thirteen acres, belonging to Mrs Sullivan and Colonel Heppesley, extending from Morehampton Road to the western boundary of Herbert Park, at a yearly rent of £400, for a term of three years.

It had already been decided that a great public meeting should be held in Dublin, for the purpose of inaugurating the Guarantee Fund intended to be formed, and Monday 22 February had been tentatively fixed on as the date. In the meantime the General Committee and various subcommittees were meeting almost daily – for instance, meetings were held on 1, 2, 4, 8 and 9 February. At these meetings deputations of members were appointed to wait on the various public companies and private firms, to proceed to Belfast, Cork, and other provincial cities, to obtain promises of cash subscriptions and guarantees, while the work of general organisation was pushed energetically ahead.

About this time it occurred to some persons, several of whom had taken a prominent part in the earlier proceedings connected with the launching of the project to hold an International Exhibition, that it was an opportune moment to set about the organisation of a national exhibition. Accordingly, several meetings were held by those who approved this idea, a committee was appointed, and a certain amount of money collected, but eventually the movement collapsed through the absence of any substantial support. However, before the impracticability of the new project was conclusively demonstrated, a certain degree of confusion and friction was generated, which somewhat embarrassed those who were endeavouring to fulfil the task entrusted to them by the Irish Industrial Conference. For instance, at the Public Meeting called in support of the Guarantee Fund, at which Sir James Murphy, Bart., president of the Chamber of Commerce, presided, several persons identified with the opposition project attended, resulting in some disturbance and regrettable scenes. As a consequence, while the work of organisation was steadily continued, progress was not so rapid as it probably would otherwise have been.

The next meeting of the committee was held on 29 March, and it at once became apparent that the opposition raised to the accomplishment of its purpose had only strengthened the determination of the members to carry it into effect. The attendance was one of the largest recorded since the formation of the committee, and the Earl of Drogheda presided. Subcommittees were appointed to finally settle the Articles of Association, and to draft a manifesto explanatory of the purposes of the Exhibition. It was further decided to send a deputation to London, and also deputations to Belfast and Cork, Liverpool and Manchester.

FORMING THE GUARANTEE FUND

Before the beginning of April 1904, while much had been done by individual effort, newspaper appeals, and by speeches at meetings of the various public bodies, to raise a Guarantee Fund sufficient in amount to justify the taking of effective steps towards the actual establishment of the Exhibition, there was nothing in the nature of a definite official organisation. This was mainly due to the fact that the committee had been, as events proved, unduly sanguine in relying on receiving liberal and practical assistance from the Treasury. Had this been forthcoming and the usual Royal Commission appointed to administer the affairs of the Exhibition, the duties of the committee would have been of a very different kind from that which they became, involving, as they did, heavy responsibility and great toil.

It was, however, daily becoming apparent that the heads of the Irish Government were evincing disinclination to give monetary aid on a scale worthy of the undertaking to which the committee was pledged. Under these circumstances it became absolutely necessary that practical steps should be taken, with as little delay as possible, to ascertain if a fund could be created sufficient in amount to justify the committee in proceeding with the establishment of the Exhibition. At a meeting held on 12 April 1904, an address, with this object in view, was unanimously approved for general circulation. In part, the document was as follows:

> At the very influential and representative meeting held in furtherance of the Irish Industrial Movement, in the Royal University, in April 1903, presided over by the Right Hon. J.W. Pirrie, DL, it was unanimously resolved to establish an Institute of Commerce and Industries in Ireland, and to hold an International Exhibition in Dublin in 1906, under the patronage of the King. His Majesty's patronage ensures the advantage of official recognition and support of the Exhibition by foreign Governments.
>
> The experience of the Executive of the Irish Institute of Commerce and Industries leads them to believe that the organisation of the Exhibition project, which would bring manufacturers and others from all parts of Ireland into close association in connection with industrial affairs during a period of two or three years, would be an admirable platform on which the more permanent work of the Institute could be built up. An association for industrial development in the South of Ireland, which is already doing good work, has been the outcome of the exhibition recently held in Cork.
>
> The committee nominated at the Royal University meeting to carry out the Exhibition project have been for some months engaged in making the preliminary arrangements in connection with the important undertaking committed to their charge.

After describing the extent of the financial support needed and the steps which had already been taken to secure it, the address proceeded:

All the work at the Exhibition will, as far as possible, be executed of Irish material by Irish workmen, and as the primary object of those who are engaged in this enterprise is the advancement of Irish Industry, a special committee will be formed, whose duty will be, amongst others, to reserve the most prominent position in the Exhibition for the display of Irish Manufactures.

If emigration is to be effectively checked, it can only be by the establishment of new, and the extension of existing manufacturing industries on a much larger scale than the markets of this country alone would demand. If this object is ever to be attained, the vision of our manufacturers, when seeking a market for their products, must not be limited by the seas which surround this island. Already certain Irish manufactures have made their way not only into English markets, but into the markets of the world, to a much greater extent than is generally supposed, and in recent years several classes of goods have been sent abroad from Ireland which were never exported before. In no way can this export trade be so much stimulated, Irish goods be so well advertised, and new markets so readily secured, as by establishing such an Exhibition as will induce the largest number of possible purchasers to come from England and other countries, when they will see what Ireland is capable of producing, prominently and effectively displayed.

In order to accomplish the truly patriotic objects they have set before them, the committee now confidently appeals to all Irishmen and friends of Ireland to join in the guarantee, and so enable them to raise the necessary funds for carrying out their great enterprise.

Not the least interesting circumstance connected with this document is that all the promises contained in the passages quoted have been fulfilled, while the general principles enunciated are as true today as when it was written.

The publication and circulation of the address at once gave a stimulus to the Guarantee Fund, while the members of the committee, divided into district or provincial deputations, exerted themselves untiringly in seeking additional subscriptions. At a meeting of the Organising Committee, held on 26 April 1904, an important announcement was made, Mr Murphy being able to state that the Right Hon. the Lord Mayor of London had accorded a warm welcome to himself and the members of the committee appointed to wait on him, and that his Lordship had promised his heartiest co-operation in making their movement a success. Encouraging news also came to hand from Belfast, where it was decided to hold a public meeting on a day to be fixed by the Lord Mayor of that city. Moreover, the actual amount of the Guarantee Fund to date was stated to be £69,870 7s 0d. A small committee was formed for the purpose of considering the advisability of appointing a paid organiser, and on the recommendation of this committee, Mr James Shanks, JP, was engaged to render special services in promoting the work of the committee in the first instance, for a period of six months.

On 5 May an important meeting was held in Belfast, under the presidency of the Lord Mayor, Sir Otto Jaffe, for the purpose of receiving a deputation from the committee. The members of this deputation were Mr W.M. Murphy, Mr James Talbot-Power, Mr Vere Ward Brown, Mr Alfred Manning, Mr John H. Ryan, and Mr Shanks. The Lord Mayor, in an eloquent speech, welcomed the representatives of Dublin, and Mr Murphy, in reply, explained at length the purposes of the Exhibition and its promoters, as well as the assurance of success already forthcoming in the amount of the Guarantee Fund. He was able to tell the meeting that:

> Up to the present time they had received guarantees in the City of Dublin alone for more than half the amount of their requirements, and they thought that, having given that evidence in Dublin of the faith they had in this undertaking by subscribing something like £75,000 without any great effort, the time had come when they might fairly and lawfully ask for the assistance of other parts of Ireland. They came with more confidence to the Northern capital, because some members of their committee had already visited Belfast and been kindly received by the Lord Mayor, and had also received promises of support, which were now being kindly and generously fulfilled.

The meeting decided to appoint a representative local committee, with the Lord Mayor as chairman, in order to obtain contributions in cash and by guarantee to the Exhibition. Henceforward, Belfast stood shoulder to shoulder with Dublin in the work of organisation.

On Wednesday 18 May 1904, a most successful meeting was held in the Mansion House, London, under the presidency of the Right Hon. the Lord Mayor, Sir James Ritchie, Bart., in support of the Exhibition.

The High Sheriffs, aldermen, and common councillors, with a large number of the leading citizens of London, were present. The Lord Mayor, in opening the proceedings, expressed his full sympathy with the project it was sought to help, and before the meeting closed, it was resolved, on the motion of Sheriff Sir Alfred Reynolds, seconded by Sir Arthur Trendell, to form a London Committee, to co-operate with the Dublin Committee in securing guarantees and other forms of support.

This committee rendered much valuable assistance in raising funds and enlisting exhibitors, while its formation undoubtedly aided in bringing home to the mind of the British public the fact that Ireland was going to have an International Exhibition. In one important section of the Exhibition – that of the Fine Arts – the technically qualified members of the committee rendered valuable assistance, while that given by Mr A.G. Temple can only be described as priceless. To that gentleman belongs the honour of having brought together, in the Art Gallery of the Exhibition, one of the noblest, as well as largest, collections of modern painting and sculpture to be seen in Europe.

In connection with the meeting in the London Mansion House, it is of special interest now to note that one of the messages of goodwill received by its organisers during the course of the proceedings was the following:

Lord and Lady Aberdeen.

Cordial good wishes, in which Lady Aberdeen joins, and sincere regrets at being unexpectedly prevented from attending today. Please present my thanks and apologies to the Lord Mayor.

Aberdeen

Thus, at an early stage in its history, the names of the Earl and Countess of Aberdeen are seen associated with an undertaking, the full accomplishment of which was to form such a gratifying incident in the records of their second Irish Viceroyalty.

The London meeting, indeed, helped in many ways to give a great impetus to the movement, while the fact that the general work of developing the guarantee fund was now in the capable and energetic hands of Mr Shanks, who, devoting himself to a laborious and often thankless task with tireless zeal, soon produced excellent results. The backbone of the Guarantee Fund, however, was made up of the subscriptions of the great carrying companies, including £12,500 from the Dublin United Tramway Company, and £5,000 each from the Great Northern and the Great Southern and Western Railway Companies.

The subscriptions of the banks and other financial institutions, moreover, were on a very generous scale, and with splendid liberality Lord Viscount Iveagh, KP, became a guarantor in the sum of £10,000, besides subscribing £1,000 in cash. The great firm of Messrs Arthur Guinness, Son, & Co., Ltd, were guarantors of £5,000. By 19 July 1904, the Guarantee Fund had reached the sum of £92,828 13s 0d, and, on 13 September, £103,270 15s 0d.

On 27 September, the functions of the various Organising Committees, which had their origin in the Irish Industrial Conference, came to an end by transference to the legally constituted body, the Irish International Exhibition (Incorporated), which had been duly approved by the Board of Trade, and registered as a limited company not formed for the purposes of personal profit.

According to the provisions of its Memorandum and Articles of Association, the Governing Body of the Irish International Exhibition (Incorporated) was its Executive Council, which was to be composed of such guarantors of at least £50, and cash subscribers of at least £10, who might signify in writing their willingness to act as members.

The Executive Council was authorised to devolve, from time to time, as it might think fit, any or all of its powers to subsidiary committees, and eventually it confided the entire conduct of the affairs of the Exhibition to the Finance and General Purposes Committee. The chairman of this committee was Mr W.M. Murphy, and its vice-chairmen – in succession – Mr John Irwin, the late Mr Vere Ward Brown, and Mr Robert Booth, JP. The Finance and General Purposes Committee was the real executive and administrative centre of the Exhibition from start to finish.

The first meeting of the Executive Council was held on 21 September 1904, and of the Finance and General Purposes Committee on 14 October 1904. Henceforward, the task to be got through was almost wholly of that plodding, laborious, collar work, which tries both endurance and patience most severely, and which can only be undertaken with any chance of permanent success by men whose temperament enables them to foresee that triumph will crown perseverance, and whose grim determination will not allow perseverance to be baulked by difficulty.

At a meeting of the Executive Council held on Wednesday 12 October 1904, Mr Joseph Ward, JP, in the chair, Mr Shanks was appointed Chief Executive Officer till the close of the Exhibition.

On 22 September 1904, the amount of the Guarantee Fund was reported as being £103,270, and from the date of his appointment in the following month, Mr Shanks engaged energetically in the work of securing further subscriptions. During the ensuing eight months, however, progress was comparatively slow, and on 24 May 1905, Mr Shanks had to recount, in a report to the Finance Committee, somewhat melancholy experiences.

According to this document the Guarantee Fund had then only increased to £106,865. However, the report was not entirely negative, for Mr Shanks was able to record in it, as the result of a visit to London, the willingness of the eminent firm of contractors, Messrs Humphreys, Ltd, Knightsbridge, London, to sign a guarantee for £25,000 – afterwards increased to £26,000 – in the event of their plans and estimates for the construction of the Exhibition buildings being approved and the contract placed with them, on terms satisfactory to the committee. The committee approved the proposed arrangement, thus raising the possible amount of the Guarantee Fund to a total of £131,865. In his report Mr Shanks declared himself confident of being able to arrange similar terms with other large contractors, and the result showed that he was not over-confident. It was largely as a result of the policy thus adopted that, on 6 September 1905, Mr Shanks was able to report to a meeting of the Finance Committee that the guarantees promised to date amounted to £150,178. A week later, on 13 September, the fund stood at £151,178. It was not,

Left: James Shanks, Chief Executive Officer.

Opposite: The Exhibition's Ballsbridge entrance.

however, until 10 January 1906, that it was possible for Mr Shanks to hand to the solicitor for the Bank of Ireland, Mr C.J. Rutherford, validly executed guarantees to the amount of £150,702. Much delay occurred, in many instances, between the receipt of promises to sign guarantees and actual signature.

The total value of the guarantees finally deposited with the bank was £153,375 5s od. It is impossible to write in terms of exaggeration of the treatment accorded the Exhibition throughout by the Chief Officers and Directors of the Bank of Ireland, without whose public-spirited and liberal co-operation the project could never have been carried out. The Exhibition (Incorporated) held other guarantees amounting to £3,250, executed in its favour, but not addressed to the bank, thus raising the full amount of the Guarantee Fund to £156,625. The story of how this large sum was raised has, necessarily, been briefly told, but its accumulation was the reward of much hard work and inflexible perseverance on the part of the Finance Committee.

SITE AND BUILDINGS – PREVIOUS IRISH EXHIBITIONS

It would have been impossible to have found a site more suitable than Herbert Park for the Exhibition. Lying in the very heart of one of the best of the residential suburbs of Dublin, and yet situated only about a mile and a half from the centre of the city, it was easily accessible from all points. The grounds were handsomely planted with fine old trees, and were eminently capable of treatment at the hands of the landscape gardener.

When transferred to the Exhibition authorities, the surface was rugged and some portions flooded with water, but within a short time the condition of things had been altered and a natural wilderness had been transformed into a beautiful park with artistically designed terraces, parterres of glowing flowers, and groves of rose bushes and other ornamental shrubs.

The total extent of the land acquired for the purposes of the Exhibition was a little over fifty-two acres, an area which contrasts instructively with that deemed necessary in the case of the two previous International Exhibitions held in Dublin, namely, those of 1853 and 1865. In the first of these the land occupied by buildings and gardens was only about two acres in extent, and, in the second, less than six. Not the least important feature of the site was that, extending as it did, from Pembroke Road at Ballsbridge, to Morehampton Road, Donnybrook, it was possible to provide two grand entrances and exits at opposite extremes of the Exhibition.

The result was that at no time, not even on the days or nights of largest attendance, was the slightest overcrowding, crushing, or other inconvenience experienced by visitors. When it is borne in mind that during the existence of the Exhibition no fewer than 2,751,113 persons passed through the turnstiles, the importance of adequate arrangements for the accommodation of visitors arriving or departing will be realised.

It may be noted that the number of persons who attended the Irish International Exhibition of 1853 was 956,295, and that of 1865, 724,958, so that, as regards attendances, as in every other respect, the Exhibition of 1907 established a record far surpassing either of its predecessors. The number of attendances recorded in the case of the Irish National Exhibition, held in the Rotunda Gardens in 1882, exclu-

The lake and the Irish Industries Section.

sive of season-ticket holders, was 261,205. In this case the receipts for season tickets was returned as £2,459, while in the case of the Irish International Exhibition of 1907, the payments for similar tickets came to £12,180, and the total payments for admission to £78,969, as against £14,575 from the same source in 1882.

It is worthy of note in this connection that Ireland has earned an honourable place in the history of exhibitions. As far back as 1834 and 1847, Exhibitions of exclusively Irish manufacture were held in Dublin, under the auspices of the Royal Dublin Society, and they proved very successful. In 1829, the desirability of such displays as an aid to commerce and industry was first pointed out and discussed in the Dublin Press.

In the year 1850, the Council of the Royal Dublin Society advanced a step and organised a small International Exhibition, which thus secured priority of the first really great International Exhibition held in London in 1851, which owed its promotion mainly to Prince Albert. This was followed by a National Exhibition held in Cork in 1852, and by the Irish International Exhibition of 1853 in Dublin. This was held on the grounds of the Royal Dublin Society facing Merrion Square, and covered not only the central portion of the space still vacant but also the land now occupied by the National Gallery of Ireland and the Science and Art Museum.

The Irish International Exhibition, promoted by the Royal Dublin Society in 1850, was, for its size, a remarkable success. During its six-month existence it was visited by some 300,000 persons. The receipts were upwards of £20,000. The Cork Exhibition of 1852 attracted 138,375 visitors, but the receipts only amounted

Contemporary poster showing the Grand Central Palace.

to £8,733. In 1858 a highly successful art exhibition was held in the Royal Dublin Society's premises.

The London International Exhibition of 1862 induced several public-spirited citizens to take counsel as to the steps to be adopted to organise a similar display in Dublin. In that year there was formed and duly registered a joint stock under-taking, entitled 'The Dublin Exhibition, Palace, and Winter Garden Company, Limited'. The capital of the concern was £50,000; the chairman was the Duke of Leinster, and the vice-chairman was the then Mr Benjamin Lee Guinness, father of Lord Ardilaun and Lord Iveagh. The purpose of the company, as explained in its prospectus, was 'to provide an Institution which will afford to the people of Dublin and its neighbourhood rational amusement, blended with instruc-tion, and thus supply a want which has long been felt'. The capital required was promptly subscribed, and the directors wisely decided that the most fit-ting inauguration of their project would be provided by the organisation of an International Exhibition to be held in 1865. This, although not productive of any monetary profit, proved, in other respects, a decided success. It was followed by the Exhibition of Arts, Industries, and Manufactures of 1872, the establishment of which was entirely due to the munificence of Lord Ardilaun and Lord Iveagh. The number of visitors was 420,000. In 1882 came the Irish National Exhibition, held in the Rotunda, which was in turn followed by the Irish International Exhibition of 1907.

The following statistics show, in tabulated form, the extent of the land devoted to the purposes of the various exhibitions held in Dublin, and the number of per-

IRISH INTERNATIONAL EXHIBITION, 1907.— LAKE AND FINE ART GALLERY

The view from the Water chute, showing the lake and the Fine Art Gallery.

sons in attendance. It will be seen that the Irish International Exhibition of 1907 was on a scale far in excess of any of its predecessors:

	Acreage	Attendance
Irish International Exhibition, 1850 (Kildare Street)	1	300,000
Irish International Exhibition, 1853 (Merrion Square)	2	956,295
Irish International Exhibition, 1865 (Earlsfort Terrace)	6	724,958
Irish International Exhibition, 1872 (Earlsfort Terrace)	6	420,000
Irish National Exhibition, 1882 (Rotunda Gardens)	3	261,205
Irish International Exhibition, 1907 (Herbert Park)	52	2,751,113

As already stated, the colossal and beautiful buildings of this greatest of Irish Exhibitions were designed and erected by Messrs Humphreys, Ltd, whose chief representative in connection with the work was Mr George Freeman. The original designs were revised from time to time on behalf of the Exhibition authorities by their consulting architects, Mr W. Kaye-Parry, MA, FRIBA, M.Inst.CE, and Mr G. Murray Ross, MA, BIA, M.Inst. CEI, who also supervised the construction of the various Palaces and Pavilions and the laying out of the park. The legal business connected with the acquirement of the site, as well as all the other legal concerns of the Exhibition, were in the capable hands of Mr George Collins, of the firm of Messrs Casey, Clay & Collins, Solicitors.

The Palace of Fine Arts.

Some idea of the magnitude of the Exhibition buildings may be gained by a brief description of each. The Grand Central Palace consisted of a pivotal octagonal hall, 200 feet in internal diameter, surmounted by a mighty dome, of steel construction, which, during the day, glistened in the rays of the sun, and at night scintillated with the flashing of thousands of vari-coloured electric lights. From the main octagon stretched out 4 radial halls, 160 feet long by 80 feet broad.

In the construction of this magnificent building, amongst other materials, no less than 48,000 cubic feet of timber, 14,000 lineal feet of sash-bars, 300 tons of constructional steel work, 70 tons galvanised iron sheets, and 22,000 superficial feet of plate glass were used.

The next most important building was the Gallery of Fine Arts, in which was housed the noble collection of paintings and statuary got together by Mr Temple, Director of the Municipal Fine Art Gallery, Guildhall, London, and the absolutely priceless collection of Irish historical relics, drawn from all the great houses of the Three Kingdoms by the exertions of Colonel Arthur Courtenay, CB, DL, to whose cultured taste and antiquarian and historical knowledge was due the fact that the precious examples of Irish art – ecclesiastical, civil, military, and industrial – the loan of which his personal influence secured, were arranged in chronological order, so as to make them intelligibly illustrative of the social and political history of Ireland. To the accomplishment of this onerous and patriotic work Colonel Courtenay devoted many months of daily and nightly labour, toiling in his capacity as honorary secretary of the Historical Committee, with a zeal far surpassing that of any paid official.

This handsome gallery was divided into seven compartments. Two of these measured 50 feet broad by 150 feet long, one 80 feet by 80 feet, two 80 feet by 50 feet, one

The Palace of Industries.

30 feet by 150 feet, and one 25 feet by 80 feet. In this latter apartment was placed the fine collection of Napoleonic relics lent and arranged by Professor T.H. Teegan and Mr N. Bonaparte-Wyse, the latter of whom devoted much time and labour to making the collection fully illustrative of the career of the great Emperor.

Not the least interesting feature in the Art Gallery was the collection of paintings by Irish artists, brought together by the gratuitous labours of Sir Walter Armstrong, Director of the National Gallery of Ireland; Mr Walter G. Strickland, Registrar, National Gallery of Ireland; Mr Patrick Vincent Duffy, Royal Hibernian Academy; and others. An attractive and valuable photographic section was also within the building. Of the Art Gallery and its contents it was well said that they alone were sufficient to justify the existence of the Exhibition.

The Palace of Industries, which was reared on the northern flank of the Central Palace, was another spacious building, measuring 300 feet by 170 feet. Here, in addition to a large variety of native and British products and manufactures, were shown the wares of Italy, New Zealand, and Japan.

The great Palace of the Mechanical Arts, which stood on the portion of the Exhibition grounds lying nearest to the Morehampton Road, or Donnybrook, was 900 feet long by 100 feet broad. Between it and the Canadian Government Pavilion stretched the noble highway, which, after the visit of the King and Queen, came to be called the Royal Avenue. This splendid carriageway ran from the Morehampton Road entrance to the Grand Central Palace, encircled it, and thence continued to the Main Entrance Hall, the Grand Concert Hall,

IRISH INTERNATIONAL EXHIBITION, 1907.—VIEW FROM DONNYBROOK ENTRANCE

The view from Donnybrook entrance.

and Popular Restaurant. It was essentially a thoroughfare suitable for great State displays, its proportions affording ample space for the marshalling of troops, the passage of a procession, and space for the accommodation of thousands of spectators.

The Main Entrance Hall was, as its name implies, the building to which the artistically designed portals of the Exhibition at the junction of Pembroke Road and Clyde Road gave access. Immediately behind the facade and turnstiles was a colonnaded space, measuring 80 feet by 80 feet, in which were various offices for the sale of tickets, for the reception of lost property, and for the accommodation of the public. From this, a gently rising covered way, 170 feet long by 40 feet broad, led to a broad plateau, from which three broad stairways and two inclined slopes granted admission to the great Celtic Court, 185 feet long by 92 feet broad.

On either side of the Main Entrance Hall, at the end nearest to the Grand Central Palace, stood the spacious Concert Hall and the more prosaic but distinctly useful Popular Restaurant. The first of these buildings (both of which were structures entirely distinct from the Entrance Hall), measured 170 feet by 80. It contained a large orchestra and organ loft. The other measured 130 feet by 80, and was fitted with all the accommodation necessary for the purposes to which it was devoted. The kitchens, larders, sculleries, and administration offices of the catering department were in immediate proximity. The managers of this department were Messrs Lyons & Co., Ltd.

The Concert Hall and Restaurant.

The Palace Restaurant was the restaurant 'de luxe' of the Exhibition. It contained a series of dining halls, one 37 feet in breadth by 70 feet in length, one 39 feet by 39 feet, one 58 feet by 27 feet, and one 42 feet by 21 feet. In this handsome structure were the apartments provided for the King and Queen in anticipation of their visit to the Exhibition. It was furnished and decorated in the highest taste, and was the fashionable rendezvous of the inhabitants of, and visitors to, Dublin throughout the lifetime of the Exhibition. Verandas and balconies afforded, in warm weather, charming opportunities for lunching, dining, or supping in the open air.

In the space between the Palace Restaurant and the Grand Central Palace stood the lofty and capacious bandstand, placed in the centre of a great circular concrete plateau, reached on three sides by broad flights of steps; on the fourth, exit from the platform to the higher level of the Royal Avenue was provided by another flight.

From the bandstand plateau an excellent view was obtainable of the spacious buildings of the Home Industries Section of the Exhibition. These consisted of two halls, one 180 feet by 40 feet, the other 70 feet by 40 feet. In immediate proximity to these were erected a model village hall, model village hospital, and model artisan's and labourer's cottages.

Among the various other buildings erected in Herbert Park were an open-air Tea Room, measuring 143 feet by 45 feet; a great Power House, sheltering the gigantic 'Dreadnought' tubular boilers, manufactured and lent to the Exhibition by Messrs Babcock and Wilcox, Ltd; an Excursionists' Dining Room; ten bars

The bandstand and the 'de luxe' Palace Restaurant.

or canteens; a number of lavatories; and a handsome suite of Executive Offices, including a Council Room. To enumerate the dimensions of these is unnecessary. It is sufficient to say that they all admirably served the purpose for which they were erected.

The Resident Engineer of the Exhibition, Mr George Marshal Harris, MICE, among his other important and onerous duties, controlled the distribution of light and power throughout the buildings and grounds. Both services were simply perfectly administered, and their excellence recognised both by the Exhibitors and the general public.

INSPECTION OF THE WORKS

By Tuesday 17 July 1906, sufficient progress had been made by the contractors with the erection of the various buildings of the Exhibition to allow of a public inspection of the works. Accordingly, a little time before the date mentioned, invitations were issued by the Most Hon. the Marquis of Ormonde, President, and the members of the Executive Council, to a large number of leading citizens, the more important guarantors, the principal exhibitors, the members of the various committees, and to the representatives of all the more important journals of Great Britain, Ireland, and the Continent. Upwards of 800 guests accepted the invitation.

The Irish Cottage, erected by McClinton's Soap, Donaghmore, proved a hit at the 1907 Exhibition and was a regular feature, expanded to the 'Irish Village', at International Exhibitions for the following decade.

Luncheon was served in the north hall or wing of the Central Palace, the building being artistically decorated with banners, flags, plants, and draperies. The programme of the day's proceedings was as follows:

12.15 p.m.   Members of Executive Council will be photographed in front of Central Hall.

12.30 p.m.   Executive Council and Guests.

12.45 p.m.   Inspection.

1.30 p.m.   Luncheon in North Hall.

The Marquis of Ormonde presided at the luncheon; the Right Hon. the Earl of Drogheda, Mr W.M. Murphy, Right Hon. Mr Justice Ross, the Hon. the Recorder, and other distinguished visitors occupying seats on either side at the principal table.

The Marquis of Ormonde, in proposing the toast of the King, stated of his personal knowledge that His Majesty wished the Exhibition success, and hoped that circumstances might enable him to visit it when completed, and, as was afterwards shown, King Edward VII remained mindful of the provisional promise thus held out for the encouragement of the promoters of a notable national undertaking.

Towards the close of the luncheon Mr Shanks made an official statement regarding the progress of the works up to that time, and referred hopefully to the prospect of their full completion within the nine months which still remained before the

The Most Hon. the Marquis of Ormonde, President of Irish Inernational Exhibition.

date of actual opening, and in doing so bore strong testimony to the good work which was being done by Mr George Freeman, the Resident Director of Messrs Humphreys, Ltd. The Chief Executive Officer further read out the names of several of the leading firms who had already made applications for space in the different sections, and gave an interesting technical description of the arrangements which were being made for the heating and lighting of the various gigantic Palaces and Pavilions in course of erection, as well as for the provision of motive power for the working of the electrical and other machinery. Finally, Mr Shanks referred to the Agricultural, Educational, Historical, Fine Art and other departments of the Exhibition, and concluded by expressing his confidence in its full success.

The first toast – that of 'The Irish International Exhibition' – was proposed, in a very eloquent speech, by Mr Justice Ross. His Lordship spoke in part as follows:

Every Irishman, said his Lordship, had, deep down in his heart, an intense desire, either himself or in concert with others – to do some good for Ireland ('hear, hear'). They all had one desire which they hoped to see gratified, and that was that Ireland should take her place amongst the other peoples of the earth as an industrial people (applause). This desire, continued his Lordship, amidst enthusiasm, has taken its most intense and remarkable form in this great Exhibition, undertaken most courageously by distinguished Irishmen for the benefit of Ireland. It was no light matter to undertake a work of that magnitude. Many were found to disparage. Many pessimists were found to say that, like many other exhibitions, it might not be a success, but he thought they had now every reason to range themselves amongst the hopeful after what they had seen that day ('hear, hear'). When the applause with which this expression of opinion was received had subsided, his Lordship said an International Exhibition had a great meaning. It called upon the people of all lands to come here and see what achievements they in Ireland had made in this century of enlightenment and progress. It asked their visitors to bring with them the best of their work that our people might see and imitate, and, perhaps, in some remote period, surpass ('hear, hear').

But the great effect of an exhibition of that kind was to stimulate the youth of the country. Without some deep feeling, without some backing of spirituality, their industry could be nothing but sordid and their achievements could not be lasting. It was, in the main, in the hope of kindling that spirit that this undertaking had been commenced.

'You will all agree with me,' he went on, 'that now whatever any Irishman might have said against the Exhibition, the time had come when they deserved, if not the active support, at all events the good will of every true Irishman' ('hear, hear').

Ireland was known as a land in which there were intense dissensions, where class warred with class, and creed with creed, but let us hope that in this undertaking there will be a broad tolerance, and that the natural kindliness of Irishmen to Irishmen may find some means of expression. Let us ask them all to give us one year of the peace of

God, that the warring voice may for one short year be stilled, to enable us to show our friends on the Continent that, whatever our history in the past, we are all capable of standing together in the furtherance of a common great object for the advantage of Ireland (applause).

In drinking the toast of the Irish International Exhibition his Lordship was sure they would all mean to do honour to the spirited and patriotic men to whose enterprise and endeavour the success of the undertaking would be due.

The toast was responded to by Mr Murphy, who, speaking as follows, said:

The duty devolved upon him, on behalf of the Executive of the Exhibition, to return thanks for the cordial reception of the toast proposed by Mr Justice Ross, in a speech of remarkable eloquence worthy of the best traditions of the profession to which he belonged ('hear, hear'). The duty of replying had been allotted to him because he happened to be the chairman of the Finance and General Purposes Committee of the Exhibition, which had done the most of the work of organisation. He was not in that position by reason of any particular desire of his own, but because he was forced into it by circumstances to which he did not now intend to allude. Circumstances arose, which caused a difficulty, and made the prospects of successfully carrying out the Exhibition unpromising and hazardous. That being so, and being, he was afraid, of a rather pugnacious nature, he took up the stand he did in order to help the undertaking to success ('hear, hear'). The more it was opposed the more he put his back into the undertaking, and with the assistance of loyal colleagues, they had now brought the Exhibition to a position in which success was assured (applause). Having done all the spade work, there was nobody connected with the undertaking who would be more ready than he to stand aside and transfer the position and all the credit and honour to somebody else.

The motives that prompted the undertaking were, he assured them, of the most disinterested character. 'We had no object in view,' he added, amidst applause, 'but the good of the country.' Ireland was, and had been for some time, in a deplorable condition. For years the people had been leaving their shores in tens of thousands, and it was evident to all that the one remedy for the dwindling population was to find employment at home for the people.

The inception of the Exhibition as a means to that end was due to Mr W.F. Dennehy, who, some two or three years ago, formed the idea of establishing a Commercial and Industrial Institute, which would embrace all the various isolated undertakings of the kind started throughout the country. The union of all these movements would make each and all of them much more effective than if they remained isolated. It was, however, found impossible to start that undertaking. Then it occurred to him and some others that if an exhibition of this kind were promoted, in the first place it would bring together a number of men, who, after working together for a few years getting to the bottom of a number of industrial enterprises, would be in a position to establish an organisation that would do permanent good for the country.

That organisation, Mr Murphy said he believed, would come and it would be one of the lasting results of that Exhibition. Another thing which he hoped would also arise from it would be to give Irishmen a wider vision in the commercial and industrial sense. One of their faults, and one of the reasons why they did not succeed, was because they took too narrow a view of the possibilities and resources of the country. There seemed to be an idea that all they had to do was to try to manufacture goods for their own people. He saw no reason, however, why Irish manufactures could not find a market in other parts of the world.

Not long since he had listened with great pleasure to a speech of Mr Arthur Chamberlain, the head of Kynoch & Co. Mr Chamberlain said that when he was thinking of coming to Ireland to establish an industry he was told it would be ruinous, and that it could not succeed. One reason assigned for that prophesy was that the Irishman could not work, that he was not amenable to discipline, and that he had too many holidays, and that he could not get on with the priests. Mr Chamberlain said his experience was that the Irishman worked quite as well as the Englishman, although he required, perhaps, a little more teaching, but he was a much pleasanter fellow to deal with than the Englishman. And as for the priests, they gave him every assistance, invited him to dinner, and, he added, my head aches still when I think of their hospitality.

They knew what had been done in the case of Kynochs'. They also had a few examples in Dublin and Belfast. For example, Jacob's Biscuit Factory sent their manufactures to every part of the globe, and last year no less than 15,000 tons were sent abroad through the port of Dublin from that concern (applause). The moral was that this and other industries which could be mentioned did not depend for their success on the demand in this country alone. The present Exhibition would have great and far-reaching results in the opening up of markets abroad for their existing industries.

There would be another result, as to which there could be no doubt, and that was that it would be of enormous benefit to the city of Dublin. In the past forty years, since the last Irish Exhibition, there had been a great improvement in the travelling facilities between Ireland and England and the Continent, and they could reasonably expect a vaster influx of visitors than had ever before reached the shores of this country (applause). The railway and shipping companies were fully alive to the value of this undertaking, and were making arrangements which would assist in attracting many thousands of strangers, whose coming could not fail to be most beneficial to the country at large and to the visitors themselves as well. They would have an opportunity of seeing not only a great Exhibition, but the beautiful scenery in and about Dublin, and of visiting beauty spots throughout Ireland which were, perhaps, not surpassed in any other part of the world.

Mr Murphy concluded with a complimentary reference to the ability and zeal displayed by the Chief Executive Officer.

Colonel Hutcheson Poë, CB, also replied to the toast, and in the course of his remarks said it had been sometimes urged that Ireland had nothing to gain and everything to lose by such an exhibition, and that they were only inviting failure by drawing comparisons between their own commodities and those of their neighbours. From such a doctrine he totally dissented. He believed the very reverse was true, and that Ireland had nothing to fear, but much to look forward to from such an exhibition as that. It was, unfortunately, true, he said, that they had few manufactures in Ireland, but it was no less true that those they had were amongst the best of their kind, and as such were perfectly able to hold their own in competition with those of a similar description produced elsewhere. But if they could claim such a high place for them they were nonetheless constrained to admit that many of them were severely handicapped by their limited output, and their restricted market, and that any means which could be devised for increasing the one and enlarging the other would be of enormous benefit. Such, at least, was the underlying idea embodied in the minds of those gentlemen who first supported the movement at the great meeting in the Royal University in 1903, when the only consideration that influenced the decision that was then arrived at by men representing every political creed and religious belief, was what would be best suited to the interests of the country, and how those interests could best be developed and advanced.

Colonel Poë closed an eloquent speech with an appeal for a display of goodwill and co-operation on the part of Irishmen of every creed and class; the sinking of little differences of opinion, the brushing aside of petty jealousies and personalities, and a united effort during the few months that yet remained on the part of everyone to do their best in the interests of the Exhibition.

Mr Alderman Irwin, in proposing the next toast – that of 'The Press' – said that the Exhibition had been undertaken, not for the benefit of any individuals, nor for the reward of any syndicate, but for the good of the country at large. They had been subjected, notwithstanding, to a certain amount of opposition, due, perhaps, to ignorance of the real motives underlying the movement; but they hoped that any little friction would ultimately disappear, and that Irishmen would come to see that this was one means of bringing them together and of showing other countries what they could produce in this little island. If there was one gentleman in the city of Dublin to whom they were indebted for the dogged perseverance with which this enterprise had been persisted, it was Mr Wm. Murphy. The toast proposed by Alderman Irwin was responded to by Comte Robert de Caix, representative of the *Journal des Débats*, Paris, and Mr W.A. Locker, editor of the *Irish Times*. The latter referred to the gratification with which he witnessed the approaching success of a project which owed its origin to a brother journalist – Mr Dennehy.

The toast of 'The Visitors' was proposed by Mr Joseph Mooney, JP, who, in the course of his remarks, said that he, for one, would not have raised his hand to help forward this project if, as an Irishman, he did not believe it would be for the general good of the country. He believed that if Irish manufacturers would endeavour to attain the success their goods merited they should not be afraid of putting them in competition with those of any other country. Mr Mooney added that he looked forward to the great success of the project, which had now reached a point which made its complete accomplishment certain. The Consul for France, M.H. Lefeuvre-Méaulle, Knight of the Legion of Honour, responded in an eloquent and graceful speech, in which he said that one effect of the Exhibition must be to make Ireland and her manufactures better known upon the Continent than they had hitherto been.

The last toast – that of the 'Most Honourable the Marquis of Ormonde, KP', President of the Irish International Exhibition, was proposed in a felicitous speech by the Honourable the Recorder of Dublin, Mr Thomas Lopdell O'Shaughnessy, KC.

Shortly afterwards the large company dispersed, many devoting much further time to closer inspection of the building operations and laying out of the grounds, and thus came to an end what may be described as the first of many agreeable and interesting ceremonies of which the Exhibition was the scene.

VISIT OF THE INSTITUTE OF JOURNALISTS

The Annual Conference of the Institute of Journalists having been announced to be held in Dublin in the early part of September 1906, the Finance and General Purposes Committee deemed the occasion an appropriate one for bringing under the notice of its members the character and extent of the work in which they were engaged. In the interval which elapsed since the first public view described in the previous chapter, much progress had been made in the construction of the buildings as well as with the laying out and planting of the grounds.

There was no longer any reason to fear that the Exhibition would not be fully completed in time for the formal opening, which had already been fixed for the following May. Accordingly, an invitation was tendered to the President and Council of the Institute to include a visit to the Exhibition in the programme of the Conference. This proposal being accepted, arrangements were made to entertain the delegates at lunch, and a number of leading citizens were invited to meet them. The function took place on Thursday 6 September.

Mr William M. Murphy presided at the luncheon, and, in proposing the toast of the King, expressed the hope that His Majesty would honour their Exhibition with his presence next year. Mr Murphy added that in the absence of the Marquis of Ormonde, who greatly regretted he was not able to be there, he was given the great honour of taking the chair and welcoming the members of the Institute of Journalists and their lady friends, a duty that gave him great personal pleasure, and he hoped that when they left the shores of Ireland they would carry away pleasant memories of their visit.

It may be noted in this connection that one of the most beautiful exhibits in the Palace of Industries, while the Exhibition was open, was that of the Galway Granite Quarry and Marble Works, Ltd. The products of this quarry rival in quality the

Inside the Palace of Industries.

finest of the great marble mines of Italy or Sicily, and its working provides a large amount of profitable employment for the people of a district who were wholly dependent on their scanty earnings as agricultural labourers previous to its development through the energy and enterprise of Colonel Courtenay.

The remainder of the afternoon was devoted by the guests to further examination of the buildings and grounds, as well as of the many ingenious mechanical contrivances employed by Messrs Humphreys to facilitate their erection. The result of the visit was to assist, through the medium of the British, Colonial, Continental, and American Presses, in bringing home to the peoples of other lands realisation of the fact that the Irish International Exhibition of 1907 had already passed from the region of mere project and was well on course to becoming that of accomplished fact.

PROGRESS AND COMPLETION

Construction of the huge Palaces and Pavilions of the Exhibition progressed steadily from start to finish, without hitch or accident of any serious kind, in the hands of Messrs Humphreys, the contractors. The magnitude of these buildings can be gathered from the details already given as to the quantities of materials employed in their erection, but the amount actually expended on them affords an even better idea of their beauty and extent. The Central Palace, with its noble dome and great bandstand, cost £33,749. The Main Entrance, at the junction of Clyde and

The Grand Central Palace.

Herbert Roads, with the covered way over Clyde Lane, the great Celtic Court, with its surrounding galleries, the Concert Hall and Popular Restaurant, cost £15,208. The Palace of the Mechanical Arts, after providing for the massive concrete beds necessary for the safe installation of the engines, dynamos, etc., required for the provision of power and light, cost £13,380. The Palace of the Fine Arts cost £7,948; the Palace of Industries, £7,991; the Palace Restaurant, £6,473; the catering offices, with kitchens and bakery, £4,785; the Irish Home Industries buildings, £2,356; the Gas Pavilion £2,523; the construction of the lake, the ornamental bridges, and the temple on the miniature island cost £3,676; while the great Water chute which towered high above the lake, cost an additional £3,241.

When it is remembered that the construction of all these edifices was being proceeded with simultaneously, or almost simultaneously, as well as that of a number of bars or canteens; the great open-air Tea Room; the Executive Offices; the Herbert Hall; the buildings for various sideshows, like the Rivers of Ireland, the Boiler House, the Cinematograph Hall; the Morehampton Road and Doctor's Walk entrances; the various lavatories, which were on a most extensive scale, and a host of other structures, some idea can be formed of the immense strain imposed on all concerned in the carrying through of a great national undertaking. The amount expended on the erection of the buildings and enclosure of the Exhibition was £118,061, but various incidental expenditures, such as that on lavatory and plumbing appliances, and hire of turnstiles, with architect's and surveyor's fees, salary of clerk of works, etc., brought the total cost to £123,604.

The expenditure on the grounds of the Exhibition was necessarily on a proportionate scale. The committee had taken over possession of Herbert Park in what was

Right: The Palace of Mechanical Arts.

Below: The Water chute in action.

practically a state of nature, and one of a very wild kind. The ground was wholly undrained; in winter or wet weather large tracts were little better than marshes or swamps. As a consequence, a sum of £3,660 had to be expended on drainage works before much could be done in the way of landscape gardening. The construction of the roads and paths cost £17,106, and, in all, the sum devoted to the development and decoration of the grounds was £25,900.

In this connection it is of interest to describe the nature of the organisation which controlled this large expenditure, as well as of that which administered the affairs of the various sections of the Exhibition. It may at once be said that if it had not been for the hearty and self-sacrificing co-operation of the members of the various committees, the Exhibition could never have been brought into existence or secured the measure of success it did. Success, it is necessary to remember, is not always gauged by the toll of monetary profit secured. Judged by such a standard, the Exhibition was itself immediately unprofitable. In reality, however, there was not one of the business subscribers to the Guarantee Fund who did not benefit commercially and financially during the period the Exhibition remained open, far in excess of the amount of liability incurred. Generous acknowledgment of this fact was publicly made by practically all the larger guarantors. Moreover, the circumstance has to be taken into account that the holding of the Exhibition conferred an enormous degree of benefit upon Dublin and Ireland generally, owing to the large number of visitors it attracted from Great Britain, the Colonies, the United States, the Continent, and elsewhere. The task of construction involved the giving of much-needed employment to a veritable host of artisans and labourers, of whom a very considerable proportion found profitable occupation again when the time for demolition came.

The Memorandum and Articles of Association of the Irish International Exhibition (Incorporated) provided that all guarantors of a sum not less than fifty pounds or subscribers of at least ten pounds in cash should be eligible for membership of the incorporated association, and should be so enrolled on signifying in writing their desire to that effect. Enrolment as a member involved acceptance of an ultimate possible liability of one pound. The Articles of Association further provided that such of the aforesaid enrolled members of the incorporated body as, again in writing, signified their willingness to serve on the Executive Council of the Exhibition should be placed thereon. The Exhibition, however, being an association incorporated under the provisions of the Companies Acts as one not carried on for purposes of profit, its members were prohibited, under serious penalties, from engaging in any business relations with it.

At an early stage in the life of the Exhibition (Incorporated), the Finance and General Purposes Committee was constituted, 'to control the business administration of the Exhibition, and to make such expenditure in furtherance of the enterprise as they may deem advisable', and, consequently, possessed practically plenary authority. Periodical meetings of the Executive Council were held, for the

R.S. Tresilian, chairman of the Accounts
Committee.

purpose of informing its members of the proceedings of the Finance Committee,
but as that body had delegated all its powers to the latter, these were mainly formal
assemblies. They, however, served the useful purpose of enabling the members of
the council to make suggestions to their colleagues of the Finance Committee as
necessity arose. The Chief Executive Officer, Mr Shanks, attended all the meetings
of the committee and council, and was an active participant in all their proceedings. Indeed, on Mr Shanks devolved the labour and responsibility of carrying on
the general business of the Exhibition from hour to hour, and of dealing with the
enormous amount of detail which could not possibly be allowed to lie over for
consideration by the committee.

The chairman, Mr Murphy, devoted himself unreservedly to the direction and
supervision of the works and general organisation of the Exhibition. Every day
witnessed some new difficulty or new emergency; constant consultations had to
be held with architects, engineers, contractors, applicants for special facilities
in the matter of exhibits, advertising, or sideshows; troubles with officials had
to be summarily settled; and generally the affairs of the Exhibition demanded
an amount of attention, thought, and supervision which few, save the chairman
of the Finance and General Purposes Committee, would have been disposed
to devote to them. In this way, however, bit by bit, the Exhibition progressed
towards completion, until at last, in its full beauty and perfection, it was possible
to throw it open to the public.

Nothing in connection with the Exhibition was more remarkable than the strict
scrutiny to which all expenditure was submitted and the general accuracy of the

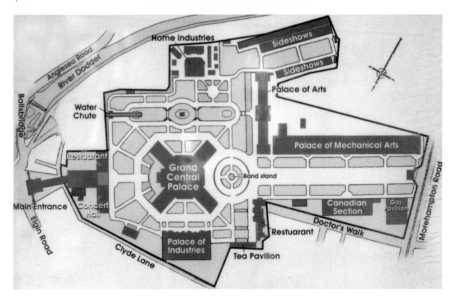

The layout of the Exhibition grounds.

accountancy department. Exhibition accountancy is almost an art in itself, so complex are the interests to be considered and the risks to be avoided, but nothing more perfect than the system pursued at Herbert Park could possibly have been devised. The result was that from beginning to end the finances and expenditure were kept under complete control.

A noteworthy factor in securing this result was the accounts subcommittee of the Finance and General Purposes Committee, which, under the chairmanship of Mr R.S. Tresilian, assembled previous to each meeting of the latter body to check all accounts and demands for payments intended to be laid before it. No cheque was ever signed, the issuing of which was not approved by Mr Tresilian and his few colleagues of the Accounts Committee. Periodical audits of all the accounts of the various departments and of the general office accounts were carried out by Messrs Craig, Gardner & Co., whose reputation as accountants and auditors needs no comment here. Thus was the security of the moneys of the Exhibition trebly secured.

THE VARIOUS SECTIONS

Unlike most other exhibitions, the arrangement of the raw and manufactured products shown at Herbert Park was not in accordance with a definite system of classification. As a result, monotony was, to a large extent, avoided, and visitors, as they passed through the Exhibition, saw, in succession, a variety of wares, instead of being compelled to devote attention for a prolonged period to the same class of goods. The system pursued, however, inevitably compels the historian of the project to deal with the exhibits in relation rather to the buildings in which they were displayed than to their distinguishing characteristics. In this connection it is of interest to note that the total amount paid by exhibitors for space was £22,886 11s 7d. The following figures show the nationalities of the exhibitors, and how essentially and overwhelmingly the Exhibition was Irish in nature, and, consequently, a useful centre of advertisement for the advancement of the interests of native commerce and industry:

Total number of Irish Exhibitors	538
Total number of French Exhibitors	278
Total number of English Exhibitors	287
Total number of Italian Exhibitors	26
Total number of Japanese Exhibitors	4
Total number of Dutch Exhibitors	4
Total number of German Exhibitors	2
Total number of Belgian Exhibitors	2
Total number of Hungarian Exhibitors	1
Total number of Armenian Exhibitors	1
Total number of Argentine Exhibitors	1
Total number of Individual Exhibitors	1,044

In addition to the exhibitors included in the foregoing table, the Governor General of Algeria, the Government of the Dominion of New Zealand, and the Agent General for the Cape of Good Hope held special national allotments of space, within which were shown a large variety of the products of their respective countries, thus adding to the total just given, a considerable number of Algerian, New Zealand, and South African exhibitors.

In attempting to describe the various sections of the Exhibition, the only possible course is to follow the arrangement of the chapters of the General Catalogue. Naturally, these commence with a recital of the contents of the Main Entrance Hall and of its avenues and galleries. In these were shown some beautiful specimens of stained glass, and of the photographer's art, as well as a remarkable collection of examples of women's work in various countries, collected for the Exhibition by Her Excellency the Countess of Aberdeen, through the medium of their respective National Councils of Women.

The principal Railway and Steam Packet Companies and the leading Dublin newspapers occupied handsome offices or kiosks in the hall, which contained a splendid reproduction of the famous Celtic Cross of Monasterboice, which,

A portion of the New Zealand exhibit.

although seventeen feet high, was carved from a single block of stone. Here,
also, were shown two ancient Irish boats, one found near Tuam and the other
in Lough Errol, not far from Acranogue. In the centre of the hall was exhibited
a remarkable model of the Battle of Waterloo, made by Captain Siborne, author
of the *History of the Campaign in France and Belgium in 1815*. The Entrance Hall
always had a gay and bustling appearance, owing to the fact that the majority
of the visitors arriving at, or departing from, the Exhibition passed through it.
Moreover, the Concert Hall, forming, as it did, a portion of the structure, was a
constant source of attraction, owing to the number and variety of the entertainments therein.

A splendid organ was erected in the Concert Hall, supplied by Messrs
Norman & Beard, Ltd, of Ferdinand Street, London, and Norwich. The technical description of this magnificent and powerful instrument will be found
in the General Catalogue of the Exhibition. It was in use daily and nightly
throughout the entire period the Exhibition was open, giving the utmost satisfaction not only to the official organist, Mr Brendan J. Rogers, and the other
distinguished organists who played upon it from time to time, but also to the
vast audiences constantly present at the recitals given each morning by Mr
Rogers. The State ceremonials at the opening and closing of the Exhibition
took place in the Concert Hall, the general music arrangements being under

The interior of the Grand Central Palace.

the control of the Musical Director of the Exhibition, Mr Barton McGuckin, the famous Operatic vocalist, whose capacity as a teacher and organiser was splendidly attested under many difficulties throughout his tenure of the office he filled so efficiently and with so much credit to himself.

From the Main Entrance Hall a broad avenue led to the eastern door of the Grand Central Palace, in the rotunda of which, under the mighty dome, was placed the principal indoor bandstand. Here, in inclement weather (and unfortunately, the summer of 1907 was a singularly unpropitious one), a series of military and civilian bands – both brass and string – performed from time to time.

Within the rotunda were also established the Government Postal and Telegraph Offices, the Exhibition Branch of the Bank of Ireland, two extensive sections of the Refreshment Department and the stalls of certain exhibitors, whose names will be found set out in the General Catalogue. In the noble radial wings of the Central Palace were shown a vast variety of exhibits, Irish, British, and foreign, including some magnificent specimens of native manufactured jewellery.

On the northern flank of the Grand Central Palace stood the Palace of Industries, containing, in its fine spacious halls, examples of the products of many countries. Here, as everywhere else throughout the Exhibition, the wares of Ireland occupied a prominent place, even though the Palace housed the exhibits

Left: Exhibition cancel,
15 August 1907.

Below: Finlays.

of Italy, New Zealand, Algeria, and Japan. The Italian Section owed its creation to the exertions of Count Lorenzo Salazar, Consul for His Majesty the King of Italy, who was capably aided in its organisation by his son, Count Demetrio Salazar, Vice-Consul.

This section was one of the most attractive in the Exhibition, and proved a constant focus of admiration from the hundreds of thousands of visitors who viewed the beautiful examples of the skill of an artistic people which it enshrined. The New Zealand Section was another noteworthy attraction. It was established under the direction of the High Commissioner for the Dominion, with the approval of his Government and of His Excellency the Governor General, Lord Plunket, who, previous to his appointment to that office, had, in his capacity as Secretary to the Viceroy of Ireland, the Earl of Dudley, constantly manifested a sympathetic interest in the project for the holding of an International Exhibition in Dublin.

The Japanese Section in the Palace of Industries contained many very beautiful and curious examples of the national art of the most progressive of the peoples of the Far East, and it is pleasant to be able to record that the Japanese merchants, who proved their commercial aptitude by taking part in the Exhibition – like all others who did so – had no reason to regret the enterprise which brought them from Tokio [sic] to Dublin.

The Palace of Mechanical Arts, which lay to the south of the Grand Central Hall, contained, as readers of the General Catalogue will be able to realise, a series of highly interesting exhibits, all illustrative of the continuous advance which the world is witnessing in the progress of modern mechanics under scientific direction. It sheltered models of the great ocean-going steamships, mammoth railway engines, magnificent saloon railway carriages, and specimens of the beautiful tramcars of the Dublin United Tramways Company. With these were shown a vast variety of electric appliances, printing machinery, bakery and cooking equipments, sanitary arrangements, and examples of the methods of organisation whereby travel is made easy and pleasant for the latter-day tourist or pilgrim to every portion of the habitable globe. In the case of this section of the Exhibition it is, again, necessary to refer the reader to the General Catalogue to enable the forming of a correct opinion as to the nature and variety of the contents of the Palace of Mechanical Arts.

The Palace of the Fine Arts, lying to the south-west of the Grand Central Palace, and its contents, have already been referred to. It contained the splendid examples of the modern British and Continental schools of painting and sculpture, collected through the exertions of Mr A.G. Temple; the beautiful and instructive Irish Historical Exhibits, brought together by Colonel Courtenay; the special Irish Art Section, mainly organised by Sir Walter Armstrong, Director of the National Gallery of Ireland, Mr Walter Strickland, his able associate, and Mr Patrick V. Duffy, of the Royal Hibernian Academy. Herein also was shown the highly interesting collection

The Palace of the Fine Arts, interior.

The Canadian Pavilion, interior.

of Napoleonic relics, assembled through the exertions of Mr N. Bonaparte-Wyse, Mr Lionel H. Bonaparte-Wyse, and Professor Teegan. The catalogue of the contents of the Palace of the Fine Arts and of its Irish Historical Section, tells the story of their beauty and worth far better than it could be told here.

The other sectional buildings of the Exhibition were the Gas Pavilion, the Canadian Government Pavilion, the French Pavilion, and the Pavilions of the Home Industries Section. In the first of these was shown a comprehensive collection of appliances used in connection with the manufacture of gas and its utilisation for domestic and industrial purposes. In the general organisation of the Gas Pavilion an active part was taken by the chairman of the Works, Lighting, and Machinery Committee of the Exhibition – Alderman W.F. Cotton, JP, DL, chairman, Alliance and Consumers' Gas Company; Mr Francis T. Cotton, Secretary and Manager of that company; Mr Robert Booth, JP, vice-chairman of the Lighting Committee; Mr R.S. Tresilian; Mr Percy Sheardown, MIEE; Mr Edward M. Murphy, and several other members of that body.

The Canadian Pavilion was erected by Messrs Humphreys, Ltd, for the Government of the Dominion. The building measured 200 feet in length by 90 in breadth. It was rectangular in form, with a floor space of 18,000 square feet. It was in the half-timbered style, with stucco, the front being broken by three gables, the central one projecting considerably and forming a large entrance hall or vestibule. The exhibits included specimens of practically all the raw and manufactured products of Canada, even stuffed specimens of her various breeds of cattle, and of the animal life of the country generally, being shown.

The Home Industries Section.

The French Pavilion was also erected by Messrs Humphreys, Ltd, to the order of Comité des Expositions a l'Etranger, whose president, Macon Barbier, took an active interest in its establishment and working. The Consul for France, M.H. Lefeuvre-Méaulle, Knight of the Legion of Honour, and the Vice-Consul, M. Andre Brouzet, devoted constant attention to the management of the section from the opening to the close.

Mr Macartney-Filgate acted as Director of the Home Industries Section, devoting himself to the work with characteristic energy, practically living within its walls throughout the whole course of the Exhibition. At the very outset, in determining the general scope of the Exhibition, the Executive Committee decided to erect and equip special buildings, and give inducements to industries of a rural nature, which could not afford to pay for space, but which, with free facilities, would be enabled to make a display creditable to Ireland and themselves.

Similar inducements were extended to such small undertakings as would be able to make headway, if so assisted. Her Excellency the Countess of Aberdeen was invited, and consented to preside over the section, aided by a committee conversant with requirements. It was realised that all branches of rural economy should, as far as possible, be included, and accordingly there were added a series of working exhibits representative of such industries as are carried on with commercial success in Ireland, together with others which might be introduced, and afford a living wage to many of our people now without work.

The French Pavilion.

IN, 1907.—FRANCE   (Copyright)

5ᵉ Aout 1907.

The arrival of the Viceregal party.

OPENING OF THE EXHIBITION

From an early hour on Saturday morning, 4 May, immense crowds assembled at the Clyde Road and Morehampton Road entrances of the Exhibition. Thanks, however, to the admirable arrangements which had been made, not the slightest confusion or disorder took place. Those who had received special invitations were conducted by the stewards to the seats allotted to them in the Concert Hall, while the season ticket holders, and others who had paid for admission, speedily sought and found points of vantage from which to view the brilliant pageant of the Viceregal procession. The Central Palace had been reserved for the reception of Their Excellencies the Lord Lieutenant and the Countess of Aberdeen, and the marshalling of the procession in the order laid down by Ulster King of Arms. Throughout, there was bright sunshine, but the day was abnormally cold, with something like a small hurricane blowing.

The scene in the Concert Hall was, in very truth, a memorable one. The decorations were on an elaborate and beautiful scale. From 10 a.m. the crowds were streaming in, and by noon the vast building was filled to its utmost capacity. Rarely before has such a gathering been witnessed in the metropolis. Here were representatives of every interest and every class in Ireland. Officers in gorgeous uniforms mingled in pleasing contrast with those who were attired in sombre morning dress, while the picturesqueness of the scene was completed by the delightful costumes of the ladies, who had gathered in their hundreds.

On the spacious orchestra platform were the band and chorus of some 600 performers, under the directorship of Mr Barton McGuckin, the leader being Mr Patrick Delany. Prior to the opening there was a grand organ recital by Mr Brendan

Barton McGuckian, Musical Director.

Rogers, the organist of the Pro-Cathedral, who gave the audience an idea of the power and sweetness of the king of instruments.

At precisely 12 p.m. the doors, which had been closed at 11.30 a.m., were thrown open, and the members of the Exhibition Executive Council and Committee entered the building. A moment later a fanfare of trumpets heralded the arrival of the Viceregal party. Their Excellencies walked up the centre of the hall, followed by their suite, amid the enthusiastic plaudits of those assembled. They were directed to chairs facing the platform, the members of the Viceregal Household and the officers and knights of the Order of St Patrick passing to places on either side.

The band welcomed with the strains of 'God Save the King', which was followed by the march, with chorus, 'Hail, Bright Abode', from *Tannhäuser*. Then came the magnificent 'Overture' to the same Wagnerian masterpiece, rendered by the orchestra, and at its conclusion there was an outburst of well-deserved applause.

His Excellency was then conducted to the platform, and the President of the Exhibition, the Most Honourable the Marquis of Ormonde, KP, read the following address, which was on vellum, and beautifully illuminated:

To His Excellency John Campbell,
Earl of Aberdeen, KT, GCMG,
Lord Lieutenant-General and General
Governor of Ireland.

We, the President, Vice-Presidents, and Executive Council of the Irish International Exhibition, desire to offer to Your Excellency and the Countess of Aberdeen a most hearty welcome, and to express our appreciation of the honour you have conferred on

The opening ceremony, 4 May 1907.

us by consenting to open the Exhibition, and by doing so with all the impressiveness and dignity that a State Ceremonial can add to such an event.

No International Exhibition has been held in Dublin since 1865, when His Royal Highness the Prince of Wales, now His Majesty King Edward VII, opened the Exhibition of that year in Earlsfort Terrace.

The Exhibition which Your Excellency inaugurates today cannot compare in extent with those of Paris, Chicago, or St Louis, but the grounds and buildings devoted to the present enterprise cover an area many times as large as the Exhibitions at Leinster Lawn in 1853, and Earlsfort Terrace in 1865.

The carrying out of this great work was rendered practicable by the aid of the large body of guarantors, whose names are recorded in the official publications. A substantial proportion of the Guarantee Fund was obtained from British sources, but the great bulk of it has been supplied by Irishmen, who think that they are serving the general interests of their country by effectively assisting a well-considered effort such as this, to promote industry and commerce.

We have every reason to anticipate that the magnitude and attractiveness of this Exhibition, and the great facilities for travelling that now exist, will draw to our shores, within the next six months, an unprecedented number of visitors from Great Britain and abroad, and we trust that they will carry away with them favourable impressions of the resources and capabilities of this country. There will be brought under the notice of this vast purchasing public the most comprehensive display of Irish goods ever got together, and the occasion should afford our manufacturers a most favourable opportunity of opening up markets outside as well as within their own country. Some of our manufacturers already obtain their share in markets of the world, and there is no reason why profitable access to these same markets may not be obtained by many others.

We entertain the confident belief that the Exhibition, as a whole, when its scope and character are fully realised, will afford satisfaction to all sections of the Irish people and to our visitors from all countries, and that the aims of its promoters will receive wide and generous appreciation.

(Signed on behalf of the Executive Council, at Herbert Park, Dublin, on the fourth day of May, nineteen hundred and seven.)

Ormonde, President.
W. M. Murphy, Chairman of Finance
and General Purposes Committee.
James Shanks, Secretary and Chief
Executive Officer.

The reading of this address by Lord Ormonde was frequently interrupted by applause, renewed at its conclusion, and again renewed when the Lord Lieutenant, moving a few steps forward from his previous position, began to reply. His Excellency said:

This address, which I receive at your hands with sincere pleasure, sets forth in eloquent and effective language the aims and purposes, and some of the chief features of the Exhibition for the inauguration of which we have assembled here to-day. It is manifest from this recital that the present enterprise is of an extremely interesting and comprehensive character. Such being the case, the communication which I shall now have the honour of reading is the more gratifying and appropriate. This is a message from the King, as follows:

'Trust that the Exhibition you are to open to-day may prove a success, and demonstrate International progress made by Ireland.'

'Edward R.'

The reading of the royal message was loudly cheered, and it was several minutes before Lord Aberdeen could proceed. When silence was restored, His Excellency continued as follows:

There is also, I think, a significance in the wording of this brief but pregnant message, indicating, as it does, the comprehensiveness in the purpose and scope of the Exhibition, especially in the combination of the International and domestic element, for the promotion of that which we all desire to forward – namely, the development

in every direction of the resources of Ireland. I cannot conclude without offering con-
gratulations regarding what we are to witness to-day as the result of a vast amount of
unremitting energy, care, and skill. In an undertaking of this magnitude it is, perhaps,
inevitable that there should be, in the preparatory stages, some divergence of opinion
as to methods of co-operation and so forth. But now that this work – this great work
– has been brought to completion, we can all unite in one common purpose, and with
one heart and voice declare our good wishes for the success of the Exhibition.

The Lord Lieutenant's reply was applauded throughout, and at its conclusion Mr
William M. Murphy, chairman of the General Purposes Committee, said:

May it please Your Excellency, on behalf of the Executive Council I have the honour
to convey to Your Excellency the request that you will be pleased to command that the
Irish International Exhibition of 1907 will be declared open, and I beg your acceptance of this key – a product of Dublin goldsmith's art – as a souvenir of a memorable
occasion.

Mr Murphy then handed His Excellency a golden key of the building, presented for
the purpose by the Corporation of Gold and Silversmiths of Ireland. After receiving this beautifully artistic souvenir, Lord Aberdeen said:

I accept with the greatest pleasure this beautiful token of an occasion which will
always be remembered by myself and so many others with peculiar pleasure and
appreciation. Certainly this exquisite specimen of Dublin art comes as an appropriate
sign and symbol of the artistic skill of the city of Dublin.

His Excellency then commanded the Ulster King of Arms to declare the Exhibition
open, and Ulster, coming forward to the front of the platform, said, 'By command
of His Excellency the Lord Lieutenant I proclaim this Exhibition open.' There was
a flourish of trumpets, accompanied by a great outburst of applause, and the opening ceremony was completed. His Excellency was then re-conducted to the chair
in front of the platform, and the 'Hallelujah Chorus' was performed by the choir
and orchestra. The Irish melody 'When Through Life Unblest We Rove', arranged
by T.R.G. Jozé, Mus.D, and the march 'Pomp and Circumstance', by Sir E. Elgar,
Mus.D, were also rendered. A few moments later, as Their Excellencies were departing, the orchestra played 'Patrick's Day' and two bars of 'God Save the King'.
    The procession left the Concert Hall in practically the same order as that in which
it had entered, but as Their Excellencies proceeded on a general tour of inspection
of the buildings, the strictly ceremonial formation was abandoned, and both Lord
and Lady Aberdeen entered into conversation with the many friends they recognised. The Gallery of the Fine Arts was visited after the Central Palace and its four
radial halls had been inspected. Here, Their Excellencies were received by Colonel

Courtenay and Mr A.G. Temple, who guided them through the beautiful building, explaining each object of interest. Leaving the Gallery in due course, visits were paid to the other sections of the Exhibition which were open for inspection.

Throughout the proceedings connected with the opening ceremony, the bands of the 1st Batt. Royal Irish Fusiliers, the 1st Batt. Worcestershire Regiment, the 11th Hussars, and the 1st Batt. Royal Berkshire Regiment played popular airs alternately, to the great gratification of the thousands of visitors who had paid for admission. The attendance of these during the day was enormous.

At the conclusion of the tour of inspection Their Excellencies proceeded to the Morehampton Road entrance, where the escort of the 11th Hussars was reformed, and they commenced the return journey to the castle at 1.45 p.m. On the way, there were large crowds at frequent intervals, and Their Excellencies were warmly greeted.

HOME INDUSTRIES SECTION OPENED

The Irish Home Industries Section was opened on Saturday 1 June, by His Excellency the Lord Lieutenant, but Lord Aberdeen's performance of the Ceremonial was preceded by an interesting function, arranged in order to enable the committee in charge of the section to offer to Her Excellency the Countess of Aberdeen a token of recognition of the splendid nature of the services she had rendered as its President, and in securing its successful organisation. The weather, unfortunately, proved extremely unpropitious, with rain falling heavily throughout the greater portion of the afternoon. It had been intended that the entire of the proceedings should take place on the village green in front of the Main Hall of the section, but complete adherence to this plan was made impossible by the continuous downpour.

Lady Aberdeen, who was attended by Lady Celia Coates, Lord Anson, ADC, and Mr Williams, ADC, arrived a few minutes after 3 p.m., and the Band of the Royal Irish Fusiliers (the 'Faugh-a-Ballaghs') struck up 'The Gay Gordons'. Her Excellency proceeded directly to the dais, which had been erected on the green, to receive an address of welcome from the committee of the section, who, with many members of the Exhibition, were present to receive her. The address was read by the Revd P.J. Dowling, CM. It was as follows:

> The event which takes place to-day is one of great significance, and, we hope, of happy augury. For the first time on Irish soil, we see a most attractive feature of a great International Exhibition – the display of those industries which are gradually assuming such importance in the life of every people. There is also to be seen an Educational Section of supreme importance, in which all who are working for the betterment of their countrymen can behold ideas to work towards; in industries, housing, developing the recreative side of country life, and bringing the advantages of modern hygiene

to the bedside of the sick. All these exhibits conjointly form a display which might be placed in any of the great exhibitions of the world, and win honour for the land of its production.

The Executives feel that such an occasion should not pass away without marking their sense of their indebtedness to Your Excellency. Since you first arrived in Ireland you have bestowed on our industrial efforts a patronage which has been productive of the highest good. The gratifying revival and development of the lace industry may be given as a noteworthy example among many such. Your name has been already associated with Irish industrial displays in various centres, particularly of Chicago, but we trust that in this section your patronage may be crowned with the greatest possible success.

It has not been an idle patronage. The section may be said to have started on the road to real success as soon as you became its President. Some of the most conspicuous features are due to your direct suggestion, and in everything your personal interest and efforts were an abiding incentive, moving all to give their best work to the undertaking. We, therefore, take this occasion of publicly expressing the great debt the committee of this section owes to Your Excellency, and of uttering the cordial hope that for many years we may enjoy your presence as a sympathetic and effective helper in the cause of Irish industry.

The document read by Fr Dowling was beautifully illuminated on vellum, in the highest style of ancient Celtic art, by Mr McConnell. On its being handed to Her Excellency, who expressed her admiration of its colouring and general design, she said:

Father Dowling and members of the committee: In reply to the very kindly address which you have been good enough to present to me, let me congratulate you with all my heart on the completion of this section, which we hope will do much to demonstrate the great advance that has been made in recent years in the variety, design, and execution of Irish Home Industries, and their strong claim to the support of all who love Ireland.

The presence of representative workers plying their various trades, showing various stages of progress, as in the case of the looms you will see employed, and that, too, in close juxtaposition to cases of finished goods, will inevitably awaken the imaginations of our visitors to consider what the cultivation of these Home Industries mean in homes where the means of subsistence are very scanty. All the supplemental industries which are, or can be, carried on in the homes of the workers, such as the making of lace and crochet and embroidery; the weaving of homespuns; the raising of poultry or bees; or the cultivation of early flowers or vegetables; have a peculiar interest, inasmuch as they cannot fail to have a great influence on the lives and characters of those who cultivate them, training them in diverse ways, and imbuing them with new hopes and ambitions, as they begin to realise the results of their labours.

This increase of hopefulness amongst the workers is one of the chief changes for good which I could not fail to note on returning to Ireland after an absence of several years. This, together with the great increase of general interest in native production and a general desire to use them and encourage them, makes the work of all industrial associations much easier than in days gone by.

The material results we see in such figures as those which show that the output of lace and crochet from Ireland is about eight times as much as it was twenty years ago, and which also show a very great increase in the sale of tweeds and homespuns, which you will see exhibited in the hall behind me.

It is a joy to me that so many of my old friends and fellow workers from our Industries Association should have come forward to take charge of this section, together with the representatives of the public departments who have helped us to carry it out. I know you will wish me to express, in your name, our hearty thanks to the Exhibition authorities, who have so cordially supported our efforts, and who have met our wishes in every way in their power. You will also wish me to express our special thanks to the Department for putting at our disposition the valuable services of Mr W. Macartney-Filgate, who has laboured in season and out of season, and who has given much of his own time and leisure towards making this section a success.

As for my own share in the work of preparation to which you are good enough to allude, the less said the better, for I have been a sad truant, though a most unwilling one, during the months when I should have been working with you. But this fact makes me all the more free to appeal to the general public to come to this section, and to ponder over its significance in relation to rural life in Ireland.

Look at the labourers' cottages, for instance. You may approve of their plan and their appearance or you may not, but at least they give a basis for discussion, and prove that dwellings of that description can be erected anywhere in Ireland for £135 apiece.

Look at the Village Hall, and look ahead a bit, and see the time when a building of this description will be considered a necessity in every village in Ireland, giving opportunities for social life and recreation, music, and lectures, and conferences, such as we hope to use our Hall here for, too.

Look at our little emergency hospital, too, and consider the comfort and help that such an institution could be in outlying parts of Ireland, allowing the district nurses to be sent out in couples, instead of singly, as at present, and giving the medical men of the district the opportunity of having their serious cases under observation and carefully nursed.

There is another exhibit to which I should like to draw special attention, and that is one indicating how we may hope that in the near future we may see schemes formulated whereby motive power can be rendered available for village trades, thereby revolutionising country life and its possibilities. And this village green which you, Ladies and Gentlemen, have inaugurated to-day, we hope to use for village sports, for contests of village bands, for Irish dances, and the like.

You may find numberless omissions in our Home Industries, you may think of many features we might have included, but the fact remains that you will find here the germs of many ideas for uplifting and beautifying country life in Ireland, even in its most outlying parts, indicating how supplemental industries can be made profitable, and demonstrating what has already been done by workers where natural quickness gives them a great advantage when trained and put in touch with the demands of the world's market. May we, then, venture to appeal to our visitors to help make this Home Industries section a success beyond our most sanguine expectations? They can do so if they will. They can note the exhibits and see where they are made, and they can ask their tradesmen to supply them with these materials or other similar ones of Irish make – and they can do this without being unfashionable nowadays. And they can, each according to his opportunity, help some Irish industry to develop, and try and brighten and help some country district by promoting its efforts to help itself. I am sure, at least, that you, Ladies and Gentlemen, will co-operate with us and give us a good start by speaking favourably of our attempts.

Again, Father Dowling, let me thank you and the members of this sectional committee very warmly. It is a very great pleasure to me to be President of this section.

Lady Aberdeen's speech, which had been punctuated by applause throughout, was concluded amid enthusiastic plaudits, evoked not only by her words, but by recognition of the steadfastness of the devotion to the cause of Irish Home Industries, which had induced her, when barely recovering from a painful rheumatic attack, to face the hardships of a most unseasonable day.

Very shortly after the conclusion of Lady Aberdeen's remarks, His Excellency the Lord Lieutenant arrived at about 3.30 p.m., accompanied by Lord Herschell, Captain the Hon. A. Hore-Ruthven, Captain Coates, and a travelling escort of the 11th (Prince Albert's Own) Hussars. His Excellency was received by the Executive of the Exhibition, his arrival being marked by the playing of 'God Save the King' by the Band of the Royal Irish Fusiliers. In the Village Hall His Excellency was received by Her Excellency, as President of the section. She welcomed Lord Aberdeen on behalf of the Committee of the Association, and hoped he would very often honour the section with his presence, His Excellency replied:

The present proceedings are of particular interest and significance, especially in view of the fact that the department or section now formally inaugurated must necessarily constitute a central and essential element in an exhibition intended to promote Irish enterprise and the development of Irish resources.

Some years ago it was not an unusual thing to hear it said that people were tired of exhibitions. Well, if there was a phase of feeling in that direction, it had passed away; at any rate, we cannot observe many signs of fatigue on the part of the public regarding this form of enterprise, certainly not in regard to our immediate surroundings; and not only so, but there is the prospect of an exhibition in London next year, and in

Scotland the year after. But, whatever may be our opinion about exhibitions in general or about any particular exhibition, there can be no doubt that the special feature which occupies us this afternoon represents a purpose, a movement, which may well form a rallying point for hearty, united co-operation and goodwill, and when alluding to the character and purpose of this section we can hardly disassociate it from that organisation which has for many years carried on a very extensive and practical work in the same cause.

I refer to the Irish Home Industries Association, and it is not without interest to recall the fact that this year is the twenty-first anniversary of the formation of that Society. One of the sources of its usefulness and success lay in the fact that at the very outset the founder of the Association took every care and precaution that it should be established on a broad basis, and thus have full scope for the comprehensive methods which have been alluded to, and the founder and President of the Society has never ceased, and never will cease, to spend time and thought in endeavouring to maintain this feature and everything else which will tend to the usefulness of the organisation. My allusions to the founder must, of course, be reserved and guarded, but having spoken of the possible connection between this section and the Irish Industries Association, it may be regarded as something more than a mere coincidence that the President of the latter is also at the head of the committee of the former. But while reference to this particular society may be permissible and appropriate, we do not forget that what we are concerned with is the promotion of the home industries in the widest sense, and, therefore, with hearty recognition of all the agencies working for that object, and representing the movement as a whole.

When the applause which followed the conclusion of Lord Aberdeen's remarks had subsided, Mr Reginald Keating, Mr E.H. Dashwood, and Mr George Freeman were presented to Their Excellencies. Mr Freeman, who had acted as architect of the section, and whose general services in connection with the erection of the Exhibition buildings have already been mentioned, handed the Countess of Aberdeen a gold key of Celtic design, manufactured by Messrs West & Son, College Green. Her Excellency, amidst applause and laughter, turning to the Lord Lieutenant, said, 'I have now the pleasure of lending you this key, which has been so kindly presented by Mr Freeman, and, on behalf of the committee, ask you to declare the Home Industries Section open. After that we will have the honour of taking you round the buildings.'

The Earl of Aberdeen, in formally declaring the Home Industries Section of the Irish International Exhibition open, jocosely remarked that he cordially accepted the loan which had been placed in his hands. They would observe that Lady Aberdeen showed prudence and care in the manner in which she entrusted it to him, but he supposed that was due to the fact that he was beginning to be found out. More merriment ensued, as if to attest the fact that the audience were determined to make the best of the situation, with the rain falling steadily all the time and the thermometer registering a winter temperature.

Escorted by the committee of the section, Their Excellencies then entered the main Industrial Hall, and Her Excellency was presented with four bouquets of flowers, tied with the Provincial colours, and tendered by girls from Leinster, Ulster, Munster, and Connaught respectively. An inspection of the exhibits was then made. The flowers offered to Lady Aberdeen were subsequently placed in a handsome silver basket of Irish design, manufactured by Messrs West to the order of the committee.

Passing on to the Arts and Crafts subsection, Their Excellencies were received at the entrance by Count Plunkett, Sir Arthur Vicars, KCVO (Ulster), and Mr J.A.C. Ruthven, in the unavoidable absence of the President, the Earl of Mayo. Count Plunkett, in the course of a short address, cordially welcomed Lord and Lady Aberdeen on behalf of the Arts and Crafts Society of Ireland. The Society had, he said, existed for some years past, and had held several important exhibitions. It aimed at elevating popular taste, and showing the connection that existed between art and industries. The difficulties in the way of Irish industrial enterprise had been trebled for the craftsman, but notwithstanding good work had been done and a refining influence introduced, due, in some measure, to the efforts of the Society, and the skill and talent of their workmen and students was fully illustrated even in the restricted space that had been placed at their disposal.

Mr P. Oswald Reeves, Hon. Sec. of the Arts and Crafts subsection, was then presented by Count Plunkett to Their Excellencies. The Lord Lieutenant, in reply, thanked the members of the Society for their kind reception, and trusted that their efforts would be attended with the greatest success.

Their Excellencies next visited the smaller Industrial Hall, after which they proceeded to the model labourers' cottages, passing en route through representative groups of carpenters, painters, and electricians. At the Village Hospital they were received by Dr T.J. Stafford, CB, Local Government Board, after which the inaugural proceedings concluded. During the time occupied in making a tour of the buildings a selection of Irish airs was played by the Band of the Royal Irish Fusiliers, under the conductorship of Mr A.J. Dunne.

VISIT TO ITALIAN SECTION

At the conclusion of the proceedings in the Home Industries Section, the Lord Lieutenant and Lady Aberdeen, accompanied by their suite, the members of the committee, and others, proceeded towards the terrace in front of the splendid Palace of the Fine Arts. At the beginning of this plateau, nearest to the Somali Village, they were greeted by the dusky inhabitants of that settlement in barbaric but friendly fashion. The men of the party were in full war attire, carrying their swords, spears, and shields, and, as the Viceregal procession approached, they brandished and clashed these accoutrements, uttering wild cries of applause and welcome.

On coming within speaking distance, Lord Aberdeen, addressing the Somali Chief, expressed his own and Lady Aberdeen's appreciation of the compliment thus paid them, and their regret that lack of knowledge of the Somali language prevented him from doing so in their own tongue.

His Excellency added, however, that he had on his staff a distinguished officer fully conversant with their dialect, whom he would ask to tell them what he had said.

Captain the Hon. A. Hore-Ruthven, VC, Aide-de-Camp, translated His Excellency's remarks for the benefit of the dusky warriors, and the chief replied briefly in the same language.

'Your Excellency,' said Captain Hore-Ruthven, turning to the Viceroy, 'the Somali villagers wish me to say that they are very pleased, indeed, to be here, to see Your Excellency, and to thank you for your kind words.' Whereat the Somali indulged in another series of whoops, which was their nearest approach to cheering, and as the Viceregal party drove away bowing and smiling, the chief urged his followers to another series of yells, which was given with energy and much brandishing of weapons.

The immediate purpose of the new progress of Their Excellencies was to inspect the Italian exhibits in the Palace of Industries, in accordance with the invitation of the Consul for His Majesty the King of Italy, Count Lorenzo Salazar. Upwards of a thousand other guests had been invited by Count Salazar to meet Their Excellencies, and, after the more formal ceremonies had concluded, all were entertained by him in the spacious and beautiful saloons of the Palace Restaurant.

A general inspection of the exhibits followed, at the conclusion of which Lord and Lady Aberdeen, with the rest of the consul's guests, proceeded to the Palace Restaurant to partake of his hospitality. On leaving the Exhibition precincts later on for the Viceregal Lodge, Their Excellencies were cordially cheered by the crowds attracted by their equipages and escorts.

OPENING OF THE FRENCH PAVILION

On Saturday 29 June, the French Pavilion was opened by His Excellency the Lord Lieutenant, on the invitation of the Consul for France, M. Lefeuvre-Méaulle, and the President of the Comité des Expositions a l'Etranger, M. Leon Barbier. The building, a very handsome one, was erected by Messrs Humphreys, Ltd, from the designs of M. de Montarnai. Lord and Lady Aberdeen arrived in the Exhibition grounds a few minutes before 4 p.m., attended by several members of the Viceregal household and a military escort.

Their Excellencies having entered the building, an address was delivered in French by M. Leon Barbier, President of the Committee, who thanked Their Excellencies

The royal visit, Kingstown, 1907.

very cordially for the great honour they had done them by consenting to perform the opening ceremony of the Pavilion. The Pavilion was modest in its dimensions, he said, and he regretted that time did not permit them to make a more imposing display. Within its limited scope, however, were to be found some of the best specimens of their industrial and other products. M. Barbier then presented Lady Aberdeen with a beautiful French fan, while Her Excellency was handed a handsome bouquet by Madame Méaulle.

The official ceremonial concluded, Their Excellencies went through the different sections of the Pavilion, inspecting the various exhibits. At the end of the inspection, Lord and Lady Aberdeen, with a large number of other guests, were entertained at tea in the Palace Restaurant by Monsieur and Madame Méaulle.

In the evening the opening of the Pavilion was signalised by a banquet, given by the Comité des Expositions a l'Etranger, to the Lord Lieutenant.

VISIT OF THE KING AND QUEEN

On the morning of Wednesday 10 July 1907, the royal yacht, escorted by cruisers, and conveying King Edward, Queen Alexandra, and the Princess Victoria, arrived in Kingstown Harbour. Immediately on the steam pinnace, conveying the King and Queen and Princess Victoria, touching the steps leading to the landing stage, the royal visitors were greeted by the Lord Lieutenant and Lady Aberdeen, who conducted them to the handsome pavilion, in which the members and officials of the Kingstown Urban District Council had assembled, in order to present a loyal address of welcome.

The royal party in Ballsbridge.

The route to the Exhibition from the Victoria Wharf, covering a total distance of five and a half miles, was via Crofton Road, Dunleary Road, Longford Terrace, Clifton Place, Monkstown Road, Blackrock Road, Booterstown, Merrion Road, Ailesbury Road, past Donnybrook Fair Green into Donnybrook, and along Morehampton Road to the Exhibition entrance.

The royal progress was one continuous triumph all the way. Kingstown, Blackrock, and Pembroke were gay with buntings and floral decorations, while immense crowds lined the roads and streets or clustered in gardens and pleasure grounds, to offer vociferous welcome. Naturally, it was at Donnybrook that the largest number of the general public, outside of those who had paid the special charge fixed for admission to the Exhibition during the ceremonial proceedings, assembled. The multitudes, which from an early hour streamed towards Donnybrook, found themselves eventually checked outside the Morehampton Road entrance to the Exhibition. This was a necessary procedure on the part of the authorities, for the immensity of the crowds coming from the direction of the city threatened to seriously impede the royal entry into Dublin. Outside the Exhibition entrance, in addition to a large force of the Metropolitan Police, fifty men of the 11th Hussars were posted, and beyond this barrier of military and police, the crowds from the city found it impossible to pass.

A wealth of ensigns and flowers, festooned from Venetian masts, garlanded all the spaces and avenues between the ivory-like Palaces and Pavilions of the Exhibition. The whole scene was bathed in a flood of sunshine, which was almost Italian in brilliancy and warmth, and those who witnessed it have not forgotten that the day

The King and Queen arrive at the exhibition.

was made notable by this fact – in a summer marred by an inclemency of temperature rarely precedented.

In accordance with the principles observed in the regulation of Court or State functions, admission to the Pavilion in which the King was to receive the address from the
Council of the Exhibition was restricted to those who had official connections with that
body. The same rule regulated the distribution of invitations to the royal luncheon in
the Palace Restaurant, which followed the presentation of the address from the council.

After entering the Exhibition grounds, the royal procession, passing down
the broad avenue from the Morehampton Road gate to the great bandstand,
proceeded around the Grand Central Palace, and, driving past the Palace of
Industries and French Pavilion, drew up before the handsome structure, which
had been erected in immediate proximity to the Palace Restaurant for the reception of Their Majesties.

Immediately the ceremonies connected with the presentation of the addresses
had concluded, the King and Queen, accompanied by those who had the honour of receiving invitations to meet Their Majesties at luncheon, proceeded to the
Palace Restaurant. This fine building had been specially decorated and furnished
for the occasion by Messrs Miller and Beatty. Over the entrance a special room had
been fitted up as His Majesty's lounge; a second had been beautifully furnished
as the Queen's drawing room, whilst retiring rooms were also provided for Their
Majesties and their suite in other parts of the buildings.

After luncheon, Their Majesties took a trip through the Exhibition, visiting first
the French Pavilion, where they were received by the consul and vice-consul for

An impressive crowd greets the royal procession upon their arrival.

France, and several members of the Committee of the section. Leaving the Pavilion after inspecting its exhibits, the royal party walked to the Italian Section in the Palace of Industries. Here the Italian Consul, Comte Salazar, was waiting to receive them. The Queen took a deep interest in the sculpture exhibited, and conversed in Italian with some of those in charge of the section.

The New Zealand Section, located in the same building, was visited next. The Hon. W.P. Reeves, the High Commissioner for New Zealand, and Mr R.H. Hooper, the New Zealand Government representative, had the honour of being presented to Their Majesties, who closely examined the exhibits, and congratulated the High Commissioner on the excellent display. A bouquet was presented to the Queen on behalf of the colony.

Other exhibits in the Palace of Industries having been inspected, Their Majesties next passed on to the Grand Central Palace, where a specially arranged programme of music was gone through, under the direction of Mr Barton McGuckin, Musical Director of the Exhibition. As Their Majesties entered the Central Hall, where there was a gathering of some thousand people, there was a hearty outburst of applause.

The orchestra numbered 120, with Mr P. Delany as leader. A choir of 300 voices sang 'Come Back to Erin', written by Sir Francis Brady, Bart., and arranged by T.R. G. Jozé, Mus.Doc.

Their Majesties followed the choir intently, and evinced their appreciation of the musical display most pointedly. As they took their departure from the Central Hall the cheering was renewed. The carriages were again entered, and the royal party

The royal party leaving the Palace Restaurant.

The avenue leading to the Grand Central Palace.

King Edward VII.

proceeded past the bandstand and the Palace of Fine Arts, through lines of military and amidst cheering crowds, to the Home Industries Section. On the way, the King and Queen were paid a remarkable tribute by the Somali villagers, who were drawn up behind the military near the southern section of the Palace of Fine Arts. The Somali were clad in spotless white robes and carried shining spears. Their chief led them in their singing of a hymnal air, to which the royal party listened, and smilingly acknowledged the kindly greeting.

At the Home Industries Section the King and Queen were received by Count Plunkett, Colonel Plunkett, Mr P. Oswald Reeves and Mr Ruthven, Treasurer of the Arts and Crafts Society. The Countess of Aberdeen showed the royal party around, and they declared themselves charmed with all they saw. Special interest was evinced in the exhibits of lace and needlework. His Majesty was pleased to accept a companion case of pipes made in Ireland, which were presented to him by the Irish Industries Association, while Her Majesty accepted a parasol from the Presentation Convent, Cork, and Princess Victoria a Youghal point-lace handkerchief.

His Majesty particularly admired a magnificent piece of pictorial enamel work, entitled 'A Falling Star', executed by Mr P. Oswald Reeves. He expressed a wish to purchase it, but Count Plunkett explained that it had already been purchased by Lady Dudley, and His Majesty then instructed that a beautiful enamelled coin-box – the work of Miss Mary Doran, of the Dublin Metropolitan School of Art – should be kept for him. Mrs Birrell, wife of the Chief Secretary, purchased a jewel casket, which was executed by Mr H.H. Wyatt.

Queen Alexandra.

Their Majesties, having gone through the Village Hospital and the working department of the Home Industries Section, went on to the Palace of Fine Arts, where they were received by Colonel Courtenay, CB, DL, and Mr A.G. Temple, who guided them through the building. Both the King and Queen were especially interested in the collection of Irish historical relics, brought together through the exertions of Colonel Courtenay. Their Majesties then proceeded to the Canadian Pavilion. Here a beautiful bouquet was handed to Her Majesty, on behalf of the Canadian Government. It was the work of the well-known florists Messrs Alex Dickson & Sons, Ltd, Dawson Street, and consisted of cattleya orchids, with lily of the valley and other choice blooms.

On leaving the Canadian Pavilion, Their Majesties, followed by their suite, re-entered the carriages-in-waiting and drove away, passing under the arch of the Morehampton Road entrance about 4 p.m., or fifteen minutes later than the time arranged. The delay was due to His Majesty's kindly disposition to linger in the different sections, and display his appreciation of the work therein.

At about six o'clock, the King and Queen left the Viceregal Lodge for Kingstown, travelling by motor car. A special launch awaited Their Majesties' arrival at the Victoria Wharf, and the royal party embarked, without delay, for the royal yacht.
At night the scene within the Exhibition and its grounds was one of extraordinary brilliancy. The crowd of visitors was enormous. The scheme of illuminations was of the most elaborate character. Myriads of fairy lights gleamed brightly all

The 1907 Exhibition by night.

over the grounds, while the architectural beauties of the Exhibition palaces were, as usual, outlined in countless numbers of electric lights. The royal monogram, interspersed with shamrocks and other devices, figured prominently in the illuminations.

Towards 10 p.m. the brilliancy of the scene was heightened by a magnificent display of fireworks by Hodsman. From the raised ground in front of the Art Gallery, rockets, Catherine wheels, and quaint devices of various kinds, worked in multi-coloured lights, shed a lurid glow on the surrounding scene, the climax being reached when, amid a scene of intense enthusiasm, realistic representations of Their Majesties were outlined in silvery lights.

The crowds cheered again and again, and the scene was one calculated to linger long in the minds of the spectators. Towards 10.30 p.m. the mighty throng began to wend its way towards the Ballsbridge exit, and for half an hour the resources of the splendid service of trams were taxed to their utmost capacity. Those who succeeded in securing even standing room on the cars considered themselves fortunate, whilst hackney cars were also largely availed of.

THE TUBERCULOSIS EXHIBITION

Not the least useful department of the Exhibition was that organised by Her Excellency the Countess of Aberdeen, under the title of 'The Tuberculosis Exhibition', which was established in the buildings of the Home Industries Section, and remained open from 12 October to 9 November.

A night-time concert in the bandstand.

The story of the foundation of the Women's National Health Association and of the formation of the Tuberculosis Exhibition within the precincts of Herbert Park under its auspices, both developments being due to the initiative of Lady Aberdeen, was well told by Sir Robert Matheson, LLD, Registrar General, in an able paper read by him during the meeting in Dublin of the British Association for the Advancement of Science in September 1908. In this address, Sir Robert Matheson quoted authoritative statistics regarding the ravages of Tuberculosis in Ireland. He declared that:

> Tuberculosis is by far the most fatal malady to which the inhabitants of our island are subject. In 1907 the deaths from all forms of tuberculous disease numbered 11,679, representing a rate of 2.7 per 1,000 of the population of Ireland estimated to the middle of the year; and they are over 15 per cent of the deaths from all causes during that year.

The Registrar General added the melancholy testimony that:

> During the eleven years 1897-1907 the total death rate from tuberculous disease varied but little, ranging from 29 per 10,000 in 1897 to 27 per 10,000 in 1907. The rates varied, however, between these limits in the intervening years, the average for the ten years 1897-1906 being 28, as compared with 27 last year.

It was in face of circumstances so sad as these that Lady Aberdeen set afoot the splendid campaign of reform which she has so bravely and successfully waged since she selected the Irish International Exhibition as the scene of her first effort to stay the ravages of a terrible disease. The story of what occurred was recounted by Sir Robert Matheson in the paper read before the British Association and we cannot do better than once more quote his words. He said:

> The appalling facts attracted, soon after her arrival in this country, the benevolent attention of our noble Vicereine. I well remember the day when she asked me for a copy of my Annual Report, and subsequently honoured me with a special interview, in which she expressed to me her determination to cope with the cause of this terrible disease and to limit its ravages. At subsequent interviews I had the honour of receiving Her Excellency's directions to prepare for her information various diagrams, maps, and statistical tables, which she considered would further the objects she had in view. In the spring of 1907 the idea of banding the women of Ireland in a Health Association presented itself to Her Excellency, who rapidly carried the idea into actual effect.
>
> The Women's National Health Association of Ireland was inaugurated by His Excellency the Lord Lieutenant at a public meeting, held on 13 March 1907, in the Royal College of Physicians, representative of all creeds and sections of the community. The objects of the Association are:
>
> 1. To arouse public opinion, and especially that of the women of Ireland, to a sense of responsibility regarding the public health.
> 2. To spread the knowledge of what may be done in every home and by every householder to guard against disease and to eradicate it when it appears.
> 3. To promote the upbringing of a healthy and vigorous race.
>
> To Lady Aberdeen occurred the idea of making the International Exhibition the first centre of practical work of the Women's National Health Association. As a result, the Tuberculosis Exhibition came into existence.

Sir Robert Matheson went on to describe its scope and results. We read as follows:

> The Exhibition was held in the Village Hall and in the Industrial Hall of the Irish Industries Section of the International Exhibition at Ballsbridge, Dublin.
>
> The exhibits were divided into four sections, viz. Statistical Section, Literary Section, Pathological Section, and Appliances Section, in which many exhibits of an instructive and convincing character were shown.
>
> The Tuberculosis Exhibition was formally opened by His Excellency the Lord Lieutenant on 12 October.
>
> On the evening preceding the opening, a lecture was delivered by Professor William Osler, MD, FRS, of Oxford, and during the period for which the Exhibition was open,

The Irish Times – A souvenir postcard.

twenty-one other lectures were delivered by experts on the Statistical and General Aspects of the Disease, on Infection, on Sanatoriums, and Consumption Dispensaries, on its Surgical and Economic Aspects, on Open Air and Healthy Breathing, on Housing in connection with Tuberculosis, and on the educational side of the question.

In addition to the lectures above noted, demonstrations were given in invalid cookery, and the pasteurisation and sterilisation of milk, on the various exhibits, and on general subjects bearing on the disease.

A conference on district nursing was held on 7 November, and the closing meeting was held on the following day, under the presidency of His Excellency the Lord Lieutenant, at which two special lectures on 'The Control of Milk and Food Supplies', and 'Certain Conditions Affecting Tuberculosis' were delivered by Sir Shirley Murphy, Medical Officer of Health, London County Council, and Dr Chalmers, Medical Officer of Health, Glasgow.

The success of the Exhibition exceeded the utmost expectations, and, notwithstanding the unfavourable weather, the lectures were attended by crowded audiences, many persons being unable to obtain admittance.

It was computed that upwards of 50,000 persons visited the Exhibition, inspected the exhibits, attended the lectures delivered, and carried back to their homes and friends salutary knowledge derived from what they had seen and heard.

IRISH INTERNATIONAL EXHIBITION, 1907.—VIEW FROM WATER CHUTE

The Grand Central Palace from the Water chute.

DAILY EVENTS

Devoted as a considerable portion of the opening day had necessarily been to ceremonial proceedings, the ordinary business of the Exhibition may be said to have commenced on Monday 6 May. The 'Daily Programme', issued at an early hour each morning by Messrs Hely, Ltd, the official printers to the undertaking, and sold throughout the buildings and grounds by a host of smartly uniformed boys, commanded a ready sale. The first page of this periodical on the day in question set forth the following list of spectacular and other attractions:

10 a.m.	Exhibition Gates open.
11 a.m.	Organ Recital in Concert Hall.
12.30 to 3 p.m.	Herr Julian Kandt and his band in the Grand Central Palace – Machinery in motion – Canadian Water chute – Switchback Railway – Helter-skelter – Indian Theatre.
3 to 5.30 p.m.	Band of the 87th Royal Irish Fusiliers.
5.30 to 8 p.m.	Herr Julian Kandt and his Band in the Grand Central Palace.
8 to 10.30 p.m.	Band of the 87th Royal Irish Fusiliers – Illumination of Grounds.
11 p.m.	Exhibition closes.

By the following day the programme of entertainments had been enlarged, as the 'Daily Programme' informed its readers. The list read:

Comic postcards were popular souvenirs.

These postcards are still popular with collectors.

10 a.m.	Exhibition Gates open.
11 a.m.	Organ Recital in Concert Hall.
12.30 to 3 p.m.	Herr Julian Kandt and his Band in the Grand Concert Hall – Machinery in motion – Canadian Water chute – Switchback Railway – Helter-skelter – Indian Theatre – Somali Village.
3 to 5.30 p.m.	Band of the 87th Royal Irish Fusiliers.
5.30 to 8 p.m.	Herr Julian Kandt and his Band in the Grand Concert Hall.
8 p.m.	Cinematograph in Grand Concert Hall.
8 to 10.30 p.m.	Band of the 87th Royal Irish Fusiliers.
9 p.m.	Cinematograph in Grand Concert Hall – Illumination of Grounds.
10 p.m.	Cinematograph in Grand Concert Hall.
11 p.m.	Exhibition closes.

In addition to musical performances, a succession of Variety or Vaudeville Entertainments was provided in the Concert Hall. Many of these were international in character, illustrative of the characteristic songs and dances of various peoples. Clever conjurors displayed their skill in sleight of hand, and marvellous rope-walkers, at once amazed and delighted crowds of spectators. Some splendid organ recitals were also given at intervals throughout the season by eminent masters of that instrument.

The total expenditure on bands and orchestras, including the amount paid for the travelling expenses of their members, was £11,220. In addition, £1,631 11s 2d was paid to variety companies of different kinds; for the hire of the organ and organist's fees, £425 15s 0d; to the Musical Director, £427 17s 6d; in Concert Hall wages and general expenditure, £339 2s 3d; in connection with the cinematograph displays, £474 13s 5d; on illuminations, £456 13s 4d; on fireworks, £450; and on wages and other expenses connected with the different sideshows attached to the Exhibition, £1,872 1s 2d. The total expenditure on the musical and other entertainments was £17,297 14s 0d. The receipts, on the other hand, were £26,258 18s 0d.

As the weeks passed by the list of entertainments at the Exhibition was gradually increased. One of the earliest issues of the 'Daily Programme' has already been quoted. It can scarcely be amiss to quote from another – that of 12 July. This read as follows:

TIMETABLE

Opening Hour

10 a.m.	Exhibition Gates
	Art and Historical Sections
	Canadian Pavilion
	French Pavilion
	Home Industries Section

10 a.m. to 10.30 p.m.   Machinery in motion

        Great Water chute, sixpence.

        Switchback Railway, threepence.

        Helter-skelter, twopence.

        Indian Theatre, sixpence.

        Somali Village, sixpence. Children, half price.

        Crystal Maze, sixpence. Children, half price.

        Ants and Bees, threepence.

        Rivers of Ireland, sixpence.

        Shooting Range.

12.30 to 3 p.m.   Band – 1st Batt. Royal Berkshire Regiment. (Programme changed daily.)

3 p.m.   Special Organ Recital. Dr Sinclair. Grand Concert Hall, sixpence.

3 to 5.30 p.m.   Band – Royal Marines (Chatham). (Programme changed daily.)

5.30 to 8 p.m.   Band – 1st Batt. Royal Berkshire Regiment. (Programme changed daily.)

6.30 to 8.30 p.m. and *7.30 to 9.30 p.m.* Ludwig's Ballad Concerts. Village Hall, Home Ind. Section, sixpence.

8 p.m.   Special Organ Recital. Dr Sinclair. Grand Concert Hall. sixpence.

8 to 10.30 p.m.   Band – Royal Marines (Chatham). (Programme changed daily.)

3, 4, 5, 6, and 7, 8, 9, 10 p.m. Cinematograph in the New Cinematograph Hall. By Films, Ltd., threepence. (Note – there is a complete change of Programme at each Cinematograph performance.)

9 p.m.   Illumination of Buildings – Special Illumination of Grounds – Fireworks.

11 p.m.   Exhibition closes.

FIRE BRIGADE AND POLICE ARRANGEMENTS

Almost from the outset of the undertaking, the Exhibition authorities had given serious attention to the question of the preservation of the beautiful buildings and their enormously valuable contents from damage by fire. With this object in view an elaborate system of high-pressure water mains, with hydrants at short intervals, was laid down throughout the grounds and within the various Palaces and Pavilions. The Finance and General Purposes Committee had, of course, full certainty that in the event of an outbreak of fire they could rely on the prompt assistance of the excellent Fire Brigade of the Pembroke Urban District Council, but, recognising

The popularity of the Exhibition was an often-embellished theme of the comic postcards.

the urgent necessity of coping with any such outbreak with the least possible delay, it was decided to organise an Exhibition Volunteer Fire Brigade composed of their own officials and employees.

In the successful accomplishment of this work the committee was aided by Mr Edward M. Murphy, who devoted a great amount of time and experience to the arrangements and discipline of the corps. By the request of the committee, Mr Murphy accepted the office of Honorary Chief of the Brigade, but the title did not do justice to his labours, which were as constant as they were practical and useful. There was nothing merely honorary or ornamental about these, and Mr Murphy was always on duty. The Brigade was as fully equipped in every respect as that of any municipality, and proved its efficiency in combating several serious fires which occurred within the precincts of the Exhibition.

Report

Owing to the material and construction of the Exhibition buildings, it is evident that if a fire obtained headway in anyone of them it would be completely destroyed with all its contents, and we, therefore, concentrated our energies on making ours essentially a preventive brigade. The efficiency of the Brigade in this respect has been fully proved by results.

In the history of exhibitions very few on so large a scale as the Irish International Exhibition escaped without one or more serious fires. Though there were ten outbreaks at Herbert Park, anyone of which might have proved serious, in every case they were promptly detected and extinguished by the Brigade.

The following is a list of the fires:

1. Outbreak under Organ Loft in Grand Concert Hall, caused by short circuit and consequent burn out of electric cables. Extinguished by hose. Considerable damage to cables, etc.
2. Fire in back part of Palace Restaurant, caused by charring of floor under a gas stove. Put out by chemical first-aid engines. Floor partially burnt and stove damaged.
3. Blaze-up of wax which was being melted and fell on spirit stove in Mazawattee Tea Stand in Palace of Industries. Put out by chemical first-aid engine. No damage.
4. Heating of flue and ignition of soot in Messrs Prior's stand in Machinery Hall. Put out by buckets. No serious damage.
5. Small fire of papers caused by heated exhaust pipe at rere of Machinery Hall. Extinguished by buckets. No damage.
6. Serious outbreak under floor of French Pavilion. Cause unknown. Two lines of hose used, one front and one rere. Joists and some flooring burnt, and hole cut in floor to get hose in.
7. Fire under floor, caused by heated exhaust pipe behind large gas engine of Power Plant in Machinery Hall. Put out by chemical first-aid engine. A very serious explosion was prevented by promptness in this case. Owing to the close proximity of the gas bags a very few seconds more would have sufficed for the flames to have reached them, with disastrous results.
8, 9 and 10. Three small blazes-up of rubbish in vacant lot at the back of Somali Village, owing to high winds in the night time. It was deemed wise to put them out owing to danger from sparks. Hose was used.

It will be noticed, to the credit of the Brigade, that great intelligence and judgment were displayed in the method employed in the extinction of each particular fire. Water at high pressure was used only where absolutely necessary. Chemical first-aid engines and buckets were used at the smaller outbreaks, with the result that 'water damage' was reduced to practically a negligible quantity.

On each firework night a number of men were stationed on the roof of the Art Gallery with chemical engines to extinguish sparks, etc., if necessary. Beyond one spent rocket falling through the glass roof of that building, however, we are happy to say, nothing happened.

Police Arrangements

The police arrangements throughout the entire existence of the Exhibition were on an extensive scale and worked admirably. They were made by the authority and under the control of the Chief Commissioner Dublin Metropolitan Police, Lt Col. Sir John Ross of Bladensburg, RCB, DL, but the actual administration and supervision lay with Superintendent Thomas Grant, chief of the E Division of the force, within whose district the Exhibition stood.

Enormous throngs of people visited the Exhibition and its grounds on several occasions, and the task of dealing with crowds of such dimensions in a safe and satisfactory manner demanded the exercise of precisely the qualities which are generally regarded as characteristic of the Dublin police officer. Not a single untoward incident arose within the Exhibition or its environs, and the fact that the action of the police aided in considerable degree to secure this was recognised by the members of the Finance and General Purposes Committee.

The following official letter from Mr J.M. Goldsmith, ISO, Secretary to the Chief Commissioner of Police, gives interesting details regarding the number of men of the force detailed for duty within the Exhibition:

DUBLIN METROPOLITAN POLICE OFFICE,
DUBLIN CASTLE,
19TH DAY OF JUNE, 1909.

SIR,

In reply to your letter of the 4th instant, I am directed by the Chief Commissioner of Police to state that the following table shows the number of Police, by months, lent to the Exhibition authorities for service within the Exhibition:

MONTH	SERGEANTS	CONSTABLES
May	25	230
June	25	235
July	27	251
August	27	247
September	25	225
October	27	243
November	8	72
December	–	15

In addition to these, a large and varying force was employed in controlling traffic, preserving order, etc., especially on the occasion of special functions.

I am,
Sir,
Your obedient Servant,
J.M. GOLDSMITH,
Secretary.

It will be seen that the largest numbers of police employed were in the months of July and August. This was due to the special arrangements rendered necessary by the royal visit in July, and by the great influx of visitors during Horse Show Week in August.

THE CLOSING CEREMONY

On Saturday 9 November, the Irish International Exhibition of 1907 was closed with stately ceremonial worthy of an undertaking whose brief existence had been made memorable by more than one brilliant pageant. The function took place in the Grand Concert Hall, which had been appropriately and beautifully deco-rated. A dais covered with scarlet cloth had been raised immediately in front of the organ, chorus and orchestra, before which bloomed a wreath of flowers and shrubs, arranged to form a parterre of fragrant loveliness. Facing the organ, on the floor of the Concert Hall, were placed two gilt Chairs of State for Their Excellencies the Lord Lieutenant and the Countess of Aberdeen. On either side of these stretched the ranges of chairs reserved for the members of the Viceregal suite and of the Executive Council of the Exhibition.

The hour fixed for the ceremonial was 4 p.m., but from about 2 p.m. the spe-cially invited guests and holders of tickets for the reserved seats had been arriving. Upwards of two thousand persons were accommodated in the hall, from which many hundreds of others were excluded due to lack of space.

At precisely 4 p.m. a fanfare of trumpets announced the arrival of the Viceregal cortège, with accompanying cavalry escort. Their Excellencies entered the Exhibition by the Morehampton Road gate, and driving down the broad thoroughfare of the Royal Avenue, passed by the southern side of the Grand Central Palace to the portals of the Celtic Hall, from which access to the Concert Hall was to be obtained. At this entrance a Guard of Honour of the 2nd Batt. Royal Scots Fusiliers, under the command of Captain McConaghy, was mounted.

On the procession reaching the entrance to the Concert Hall a great fanfare of trumpets rang out from the platform to announce the approach of the distinguished party. Before proceeding up the central passage of the hall, Their Excellencies were presented with beautifully designed copies of the musical programme executed in satin. The procession up the hall then commenced to the strains of 'God Save the King'. The doors were closed, and the audience waited for the conclusion of the anthem to give vent to loud and enthusiastic cheers. On Their Excellencies ascending the dais, a beautiful bouquet was presented to the Countess of Aberdeen by Miss Murphy, daughter of Mr W.M. Murphy. The cheers were renewed as the party took their seats, and then the orchestra gave a fine rendering of the march

Hongroise 'Răkóczy' (Berlioz), under the direction of Mr Barton McGuckin, the Musical Director.

At the conclusion of the overture, 'Die Meistersinger' (Wagner), which so often charmed the Exhibition audiences when played by the bands during the previous six months, the following address and report were presented by the Marquis of Ormonde, President of the Exhibition, to Their Excellencies:

To Their Excellencies the Earl of Aberdeen, Lord Lieutenant of Ireland, and the Countess of Aberdeen:

May it please your Excellencies – The Executive Council of the Irish International Exhibition have the honour to welcome your Excellencies to the performance of the closing ceremony connected with the important undertaking which they have now brought to a successful conclusion.

Since the auspicious opening of the Exhibition by your Excellencies on 4 May last, it has been visited by a great concourse of people, numbering in the aggregate nearly two million and three-quarters, and it is a source of gratification to the Executive to know that the result of their efforts has received universal praise and admiration from all who have seen the beautiful grounds and buildings which surround us and the treasures which they contain, and that all the main objects which the promoters of the enterprise had set before them have been fully realised.

The Exhibition has been the means of inducing large numbers to visit Ireland from Great Britain and abroad, especially from the United States of America, and as Irish-manufactured goods occupied a predominant position in most of the sections of the Exhibition, the productions of this country were brought prominently under the notice of the visitors from all parts of the world who would not otherwise have seen them. It is hoped and believed that the enterprise of our manufacturers will follow up this advantage, and find even outside of Ireland, as well as in our country an increasing demand for the work of Irish hands.

The Executive Council, therefore, record with satisfaction their sense of the advantages conferred on Ireland by the holding of the Exhibition in the promotion of more intimate business relations with other countries, which must be accompanied by immediate or prospective increase in the commercial prosperity of the nation.

Of one thing the council are quite certain, with the best means of knowledge on the subject – viz. that the apprehensions, which were at one time expressed by some people, of possible injury to the trade or industry of the country by the holding of this Exhibition, have not been justified in the very least degree by the result.

The Executive Council have received tangible evidence of the practical usefulness of the Exhibition to Dublin, in an especial manner by the large increase in many branches of business in this city for the past six months, far exceeding, as the council have reason to believe, the whole expenditure on the Exhibition itself.

Not the least of the benefits due to the Exhibition were those conferred upon considerable numbers of working people, to whom well-paid employment was afforded on the construction of the buildings and laying out of the grounds during a period of more than usual depression. Since the Exhibition opened, payments averaging more than £2,000 per week were made for salaries and wages to the large staff of officials, attendants, and other workers constantly employed in its buildings and grounds, exclusive of the money paid to the exhibitors' employees; which also amounted to a considerable sum.

Not the least gratifying feature connected with our undertaking was the large number of persons of all classes who, availing of the facilities afforded by the various railway companies, were enabled to visit the Exhibition from every part of Ireland.

Finally, the Executive Council desire to offer your Excellencies the expression of their profound sense of the indebtedness which has been laid upon them, as well as on the people of Ireland, by the kindly and unremitting solicitude for the success of the Exhibition manifested by your Excellencies.

Signed on behalf of the Executive Council,
ORMONDE,
President.
9 November, 1907.

The reading of this address and report by the Marquis of Ormonde was frequently interrupted by applause, which was renewed again and again at its conclusion.

The Lord Lieutenant having accepted, amidst applause, the copy of the address and report read by the Marquis of Ormonde, proceeded to reply.

His Excellency, who used no written notes, spoke as follows:

Lord Ormonde, ladies and gentlemen, we have listened to the reading of this address with peculiar interest; and I am very sure that you and your colleagues have full reason to be congratulated upon the success which has attended this undertaking; and when we speak of success we most certainly include, as you have done in this report, the notable and auspicious visit of Their Majesties the King and Queen (applause). That visit, as you justly observe, was primarily arranged in order that Their Majesties might have the opportunity of visiting this Exhibition, and we know how well founded are your observations regarding the impression which was made upon Their Majesties' minds, and which they cordially expressed.

It is also a great reason for satisfaction that so large a number of persons, not only from Dublin, but from all parts of Ireland, had an opportunity of visiting this display, and it is quite certain that if the weather had not been so unusually – you might say abnormally – unpropitious, the number of visitors would have been very much greater ('hear, hear'). However, no one will attach any responsibility to the management for that (laughter).

We can well believe that Lord Ormonde and the Executive and all concerned in this enterprise have been the recipients of many felicitations and assurances of pleasure and satisfaction. I notice with particular interest the allusion you, in your report, make to the Home Industries division of your Exhibition. That it should have been a success is a significant as well as a happy circumstance, and I cannot help alluding also to the fact that that section of the Exhibition has been utilised for the holding of demonstrations in that movement against the fell disease of tuberculosis, utilised through the courtesy of the Executive of the Exhibition, so that I for one believe that that spot will hereafter be regarded as the nucleus of a movement of far-reaching and inestimable value to the whole country.

'There were,' His Excellency continued, 'many features which had characterised the Exhibition as a whole. It was impossible to allude to them all in an address, or in a reply to an address, to cover anything like the whole ground suggested. But he would like to be allowed to allude to the musical portion of the arrangements throughout the Exhibition (*applause*). It was quite evident that a great amount of care and thought had been bestowed upon those arrangements, and that the aim and purpose had been to provide a musical programme throughout which, while of such a kind as to be appreciated by the public as a whole, had invariably maintained a high-class character' (*applause*). 'We may be very sure,' remarked His Excellency, 'indeed we have observed that the music has been listened to with delight by vast numbers of people' (*applause*).

The excellent police arrangements also won a tribute from His Excellency – not that the police were wanted, said he, except to make a fine appearance. It was a matter of pride, and was most satisfactory that there would not be any occasion for the police to intervene in an authoritative manner. This was not the first, nor would it be the last, time when the people of Dublin would show how they could maintain their reputation of knowing how to enjoy themselves without interfering with the enjoyment of others (*applause*).

'Many after this day,' he went on, 'will miss the agreeable, instructive, and cheerful resort which has been provided for the people in these grounds ('*hear, hear*'), and one cannot help hoping that some sort of similar provision will either be maintained or devised for the people ('*hear, hear*'). Now that it is drawing to the inevitable conclusion, the remark may be permissible that in an enterprise of this magnitude it was perhaps inevitable, especially in the early stages of the organisation, that there should have been divergences of opinion as to the best method and procedure for carrying out such an undertaking as this. Well the report states, I have no doubt with good reason, that as to any misgivings or forebodings regarding the influence of the Exhibition in certain directions, these misgivings have happily not been fulfilled ('*hear, hear*').'

His Excellency ventured to hope that those who felt these misgivings would, now that the Exhibition was to be an historic fact, exercise impartiality, and see that it merited the favourable eye of the historian, while at the same time those who had conducted the Exhibition would, he was sure, be the first to recognise that, as they had been actuated only by motives of public spirit and desire for the welfare of the country, others not able to see eye to eye with them had been influenced by the same feelings of public spirit ('*hear, hear*').

His Excellency next referred to the magnificent musical treat which had delighted them that afternoon, and said they were privileged to have seen such a delightful gathering of what he might call the musical elite of Dublin and to listen to the result ('*hear, hear*').

'Though I am reluctant to utter the farewell words, I must do so, and I accompany them with an assurance on the part of the Countess of Aberdeen and myself of our special appreciation of the unvaried courtesy and consideration which we have experienced on every occasion that we have visited the Exhibition. That applies to the highest official as to the humblest.

I will not attempt to single out names which, of course, naturally occur conspicuously to our minds and to the minds of all. We have always and invariably, whenever we have arrived within the gates, been made to feel that we were welcome and at home, and indeed we have learned to regard as friends many whose names I cannot profess to be acquainted with, but whose personality will remain as a pleasant memory.' Concluding, His Excellency said, 'I again congratulate you, Lord Ormonde, and all the Chairmen and representatives of the various sections and departments, and in again expressing thanks for the kindly greetings offered to Lady Aberdeen and myself, I would say, in the words of an old phrase adopted as a motto by the City of Aberdeen:
'Happy to meet, Sorry to part, Hope to meet again.' (*Applause*)

At the request of the Marquis of Ormonde, the Earl of Aberdeen proclaimed the formal closing of the Exhibition in the following words, 'As requested by the President of the Exhibition, it is now – I will not say my privilege, but my duty, to declare this Exhibition closed.'

When the silver trumpets of the Coldstream Guards sounded the final fanfare, the Lord Lieutenant and the Countess of Aberdeen, preceded by the Viceregal staff, and accompanied by the Marquis of Ormonde, and the members of the Executive Council, passed down the central passage of the Concert Hall, which reverberated with the echoes of that stately anthem, 'God Save the King', sung as it was not only by the 800 members of the chorus, but also by most of the 2,000 occupants of the body of the building. The effect can only be described as magnificent, and was a fitting and worthy conclusion to an impressive ceremonial.

Outside the Concert Hall Their Excellencies were received with much enthusiasm on their way to the awaiting carriages, but before entering these Mr E. Travers, the Chief Steward and planner of the seating arrangements, as well as the other stewards who so efficiently aided him; Messrs Narramore, Mallett, Pratt, Phillips, Thompson, Walsh, Jeeves, Harris, McVittie, and Major Harrell were, by Their Excellencies request, presented to them.

Preceded by their cavalry and horse-police escort, Their Excellencies took leave of the brilliant scene amidst loud cheering and handkerchief-waving all along the

The Lovers' Walk
at the Exhibition

'The Lovers' Walk'.

route to the Morehampton Road exit, a striking effect being presented by the flashing swords and brilliant uniforms of the escort beneath the electric lights of the Exhibition.

Although the formal closing of the Exhibition took place under circumstances of such brilliancy as have been described, it had been decided that the large number of visitors, more than 20,000, who crowded the grounds and buildings, should be afforded a final evening's entertainment.

The popularity of the Exhibition amongst all classes was never better demonstrated than by the crowd within the grounds at 6 p.m. The fashionable throng in attendance at the closing ceremony had at that hour just emerged from the Concert Hall, and swarmed through the avenues to the Central Palace to take a parting look at the grounds. Just then, too, there was a constant stream of visitors arriving from the Ballsbridge and Donnybrook entrances. The working classes were in strong evidence, and there were many visitors from the provinces, who also joined in one of the most notable gatherings ever brought together in Dublin.

One journalistic observer of the scene told how a thrill of excitement stirred the vast crowd which thronged the avenues and buildings of the Exhibition. A representative of the *Irish Independent* wrote, 'The idea uppermost in the minds of all was that of taking a farewell glance at scenes which to nearly all had become familiar within the past six months.'

It was no wonder, then, to find the Industrial and Machinery Hall and other centres of attraction in the Exhibition crowded by visitors, many of whom purchased souvenirs of the great event. The sideshows, too, came in for an extensive patronage.

When the visitors had 'done the rounds', and satisfied themselves that they had taken their parting look of the grounds, they literally swarmed into the Central Hall and into the Concert Hall. In the former place, Ireland's Own Band performed a selection of music both in the afternoon and evening, while at the conclusion of the official closing ceremony, Herr Kandt's band played an attractive farewell programme, in which were included some of those delightfully catchy items so popular with the afternoon audiences for the last month. 'Standing-room only' was the order during this performance, which wound up with a fine rendering of the 'Ireland Ever' finale.

While scenes such as these were being witnessed throughout the Exhibition, the Palace and Popular Restaurants were filled by hosts of guests partaking of the last repasts ever to be served within them. In the Royal Room of the former beautiful structure, the members of the Finance and General Purposes Committee of the Executive Council of the Exhibition entertained their chairman, Mr William M. Murphy, at dinner. The chair was occupied by Mr Robert Booth, JP, vice-chairman of the committee, who, in proposing the health of the guest, said that the compliment they were paying Mr Murphy was a very inadequate recognition of services fraught with permanent national advantages.

The toast was supported by several other members of the committee, who declared that if it had not been for the wholehearted manner in which Mr Murphy devoted his great abilities to the establishment and organisation of the Exhibition, it would never have come into existence, nor Ireland or Dublin reaped the benefits it had conferred.

Mr Murphy responded in a graceful speech, saying that he undertook the work referred to solely through the realisation of the existence of urgent patriotic obligation, and with a view to overcoming an unreasoning opposition, which, if it could triumph, would prove fatal to the self-respect and prosperity of the people.

The compliment thus paid the chairman of the Finance and General Purposes Committee was only a fitting tribute to the zeal and self-sacrificing labour which alone had made the establishment of the Exhibition possible.

As the actual closing hour of the Exhibition approached the vast assemblage within its precincts began to disperse. Visitors of the more elderly and staid type departed, regretting that they had seen the last of a great national undertaking, which had been not only a centre of artistic and industrial education, but also one of social enjoyment. The more juvenile members of the crowd expressed their feelings in a more vociferous and less restrained manner, but nothing occurred which, in even the least degree, marred the splendid record referred to by the Lord Lieutenant earlier in the day. From the opening to the closing of the Exhibition not a single incident occurred detrimental to the good repute of our people or of the thousands of their guests who from distant lands visited Herbert Park.

NUMBERS OF PERSONS EMPLOYED

It would scarcely be fitting that this Record should conclude without some statement as to the amount of employment the Irish International Exhibition of 1907 provided for various classes of workers. On this point the following statements by the principal contractors engaged in the construction of the buildings will be found interesting:

KNIGHTSBRIDGE,
LONDON, S.W.,
19 June, 1909.

Dear Sir,

We are in receipt of your communication of the 17th instant, and in reply beg to say that the largest number of men employed during the term of the Exhibition in one week by us was 1,600, the average number per week throughout the whole of the job being 400.

The approximate total amount of wages was £35,000.

If there is any further information you require we shall be pleased to supply same on hearing from you.

Yours faithfully,
HUMPHREYS, LTD

5 CLANWILLIAM PLACE,
DUBLIN,
22 June, 1909.

Dear Sir,

In reply to yours of the 17th inst., we send you as under particulars you require:

Total wages paid, £9,500; average number of men employed per week during contract, 100; Plaster used for manufacture of fibrous plaster, 1,100 tons; Canvas used for manufacturing fibrous plaster, 250,000 yds; Timber used in casting fibrous plaster, 70,000 ft lin.

If there is any further information you require kindly let us know and we will be pleased to let you have same.

Yours truly,
(For GEORGE ROME & Co.)

ALEX MALCOLM
SOUTH GREAT GEORGES STREET,
DUBLIN,
22 June, 1909.

Dear Sir,

In reply to your esteemed favour of 17th inst., during the construction of the Exhibition we had at times as many as 200 painters, 150 plumbers and over 100 carpenters working exclusively for the Exhibition. We also supplied and glazed over 200 tons of rolled plate glass, and this work gave a large number of glaziers and helpers close on 12 months' continuous work.

Yours faithfully,
THOS. DOCKRELL, SONS & Co., LTD

Messrs Wm. Coates & Co., Leinster Street and Belfast, the Contractors for the electric equipment of the Exhibition, replied as follows:

At one time we had as many as eighty men employed, and for a long period the number was fifty or more.

W.C. & SON, LTD
19/6/09

Above: The Water chute: the longest that had ever been constructed in the country.

Right: The Helter-skelter Lighthouse.

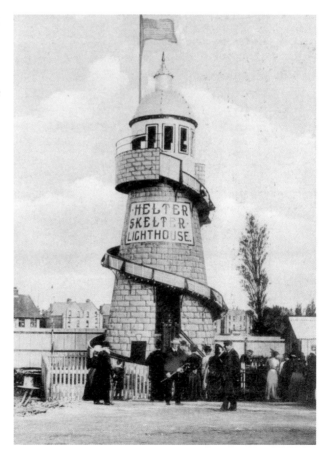

The foregoing letters refer, of course, exclusively to the workers employed in the construction and decoration of the buildings and grounds previous to the opening of the Exhibition, and whose places were then taken by another huge detachment of the Army of Labour, in the direct service and pay of the Exhibition authorities. This was composed as follows:

Clerks in general offices	27
Clerks in cashier's office	9
Grounds (gardeners, etc.)	27
In charge turnstiles, and watchmen	65
Engineers	29
Assistants – lavatories and cloakrooms	37
Carpenters and labourers	74
Firemen	42
Home Industries workers	24
Sideshows, etc.	51
Concert and cinematograph halls	12
	397
Catering department:	
Administration and office (clerks, superintendents, chefs, etc.)	44
Waiters	99
General, including waitresses	398
	541
Total	938

Thus, nearly 1,000 persons were employed daily, and in receipt of good salaries and wages from the opening to the closing of the Exhibition. In addition, however, to those just enumerated must be added the 2,600 Stall Attendants, whom the various exhibitors found it necessary to employ to look after their interests in connection with their exhibits. Thus, no fewer than 3,538 persons daily found remunerative and pleasant employment within the precincts of the Exhibition. The total amount paid in salaries and wages to the Exhibition staff proper was £23,057 7s 6d.

AMUSEMENTS AND ENTERTAINMENTS

Water chute
The Executive erected a Water chute similar in structure to those that have been put

Right:
The sideshows.

Below:
The Somali
Village.

up in the Earls Court Exhibitions and have proved so popular every year, and are still a source of amusement and sensation to visitors. It may be of interest to note that this chute is the longest that has ever been built in the United Kingdom.

Switchback Railway

The Switchback Railway has been erected in the west end of the grounds, and should prove as great an attraction in Dublin as it has done for the twenty years that it has been one of the main attractions of all important exhibitions. The Down-and-up Railway, which requires neither steam nor electricity, but merely passengers, is sure to be well patronised.

Helter-skelter Lighthouse
In concave contour, rising over 50 feet from the ground, the Helter-skelter Lighthouse encourages you to walk up the steps to its summit. There, seated on mats, a spiral slide slips one nearly 200 feet around the Lighthouse from apex to base in nine seconds, to the enjoyment of both slider and onlooker.

Indian Theatre
This unique attraction is situated between the Switchback and Helter-skelter Lighthouse, and during the run of the Exhibition, daily varied programmes, illustrative of Indian juggling and conjuring, will be given at frequent intervals by Ebrahims Sahib's Indian Fakirs.

Somali Village
A party of Somalis has been imported from British Somaliland, which is situated in the north-east of Africa. This village has been erected to represent the huts in which the natives live in their country. A schoolroom has also been built in which Somali children will be taught their lessons. Somalis are a nomadic race, and live chiefly by the rearing of herds of goats and sheep. They are Mohammedans by religion.

Shooting Jungle
A large and well-arranged Shooting Jungle, combining all the latest devices to give lifelike representations of animals in their natural state, has been erected in the east end of the grounds.

Rivers of Ireland
A picturesque front forms the entrance to the Rivers of Ireland, where a never-ceasing silvery stream bears voyagers in boats through tunnels, on each side of which are openings which represent some of the most beautiful and striking glimpses of the exquisite scenery with which Ireland has been blessed. This forms a most attractive resort for both the old and the young who delight in its original effects.

Crystal Maze
The smiles and laughter of those coming from the Crystal Maze, which includes a large set of merry and distorting mirrors, easily locate that pleasure house, and no description of the whimsical sights to be seen within could give an idea of the reality.

Royal Exhibition of Working Ants and Bees
Exhibited by Mrs Grace Burns, Earls Court, London. Illuminated and magnified, showing queens' attendants, workers, cows, and domestics, etc., in an ant city.

The bees are shown in a large observatory hive with their queens and workers engaged in their various duties of attending the queen, feeding the young, gathering pollen and honey, making wax, etc.

Cinematograph

Daily exhibitions of pictures are given in the Grand Concert Hall. Every endeavour is made to obtain the most up-to-date films, to put the world before visitors, to present a realistic series of history-making film subjects and great national spectacles.

CATALOGUE OF IRISH HISTORICAL LOAN COLLECTION AND NAPOLEONIC RELICS

Introduction

To illustrate the history of the past there are two important collections – the Irish and the Napoleonic.

The Irish Historical Section, arranged principally in the Fine Arts Galleries, illustrates the glorious past of this country, and must be deeply interesting to all who feel a legitimate pride in the story of Ireland and in the careers of her many distinguished sons – some in the land of their birth, others in widely scattered regions in all parts of the globe.

This collection is, therefore, mainly an exhibition of souvenirs of important events in our history, or of persons of Irish birth or descent who are noted in history, or who by their talents have shed lustre upon their native land.

Tattered colours and weapons of various kinds are records of the troublous times through which Ireland has more than once passed.

To this collection, rare and valuable objects have been contributed by many public bodies, such as the Corporations of Belfast and Londonderry; Trinity College, Dublin; the Dublin Museum; the Royal Irish Academy; the Royal United Service Institution, Whitehall; and the Victoria and Albert Museum, South Kensington. Many noblemen and other distinguished owners of priceless heirlooms have also generously consented to lend them for this section.

These relics of the past in Ireland belong generally to Medieval, Tudor and later times, but two remarkable objects are far older: the immense dug-out canoe, wrought from a great oak of the primeval forest thousands of years ago, and the cast of the High Cross at Monasterboice, 17 ft high, cut out of one block of stone, is proof of the true artistic feeling and the skill of Irishmen of early Christian days.

After these come relics of the days of the Plantagenets and Tudors, of King Charles and Cromwell, of King James and of William of Orange, and so on down to the time of Queen Victoria, of whom there is an interesting souvenir – the canopy held over the young Queen at her Coronation.

In the artistic handicrafts and manufactures Ireland has held a proud position, especially as regards silver and glass, and the collection of examples, chiefly of the eighteenth century, of these beautiful crafts will show to connoisseurs how well deserved is this pre-eminence. A few pieces of old Irish furniture and musical instruments show that here also this country has little to fear from comparison with any rivals.

So many Irishmen distinguished themselves under Napoleon in the Grand Armée that a separate collection has been made of souvenirs of these, and in this work the committee have had the assistance of distinguished Frenchmen connected to this country by ties of kindred or of sympathy.

The Historical Collections are classified as follows:

I.   Relics of times previous to the eighteenth century, including those of the Siege of Derry and of the Battle of the Boyne.
II.   Relics of the eighteenth century, including those of the Rebellion of 1798.
III.   Relics of the nineteenth century.
IV.   Specimens of those branches of Irish manufacture for which Ireland is noted – Old Silver Plate, Cut-glass (Waterford and Cork), Musical Instruments, Weapons, Coins, Jewellery and Miniatures, early Book-bindings, etc.
V.   Paintings and Portraits in oil of distinguished Irishmen and women.
VI.   Prints and Engravings of the same, and old Maps and Charts.
VII.   Busts of distinguished Irishmen.
VIII.   Napoleonic Collection, including objects relating to the Battle of Waterloo and the armies that took part in it.
IX.   Bernadotte Collection, including objects, pictures, and engravings relating to Napoleon's great general – the founder of the Swedish dynasty.

ARTHUR H. COURTENAY, Colonel,
Hon. Secretary.
NAPOLEONIC COLLECTION

IRISH INTERNATIONAL EXHIBITION (INCORPORATED)

STATEMENT OF INCOME AND EXPENDITURE FROM 10 JULY 1903 TO 14 MAY 1909.

INCOME			EXPENDITURE	
		£/s/d		£/s/d
I. Admissions, per Schedule I		78,981/0/10	I. Buildings and Grounds, per Schedule VII	151,604/19/6
2. Space		22,886/11/7	2. Catering Department, per Schedule VIII	80,832/4/11
3. Sideshows and Entertainments, per Schedule II		26,258/18/0	3. General Administration, per Schedule IX	54,715/2/1½
4. Catering Department:			4. Engineer's Department, per Schedule X	23,428/8/9
Gross Drawings	75,976/10/5		5. Music, Entertainments and Attractions, per Schedule XI	17,333/17/10½
Advertising Concessions	4,307/13/9	80,284/4/2	6. Fine Arts Section, per Schedule XII	6,637/17/3

5. Printing and other concessions, per Schedule III		5,551/9/7	7. Historical Section, per Schedule XIII	1,168/1/9½
6. Receipts from Exhibitors, per Schedule IV		5,073/5/7	8. Home Industries Section, per Schedule XIV	1,182/16/3
7. Realisation Account, per Schedule V		20,202/16/3½	9. Plant, Fittings and Office Furniture, per Schedule XV	3,409/8/4
8. Miscellaneous Receipts, per Schedule VI		1,950/4/10		
Balance, being in excess of Expenditure over Income		99,124/5/11		
		£340,312 16s 9½d		£340,312 16s 9½d

		£/s/d		£/s/d
Amount payable by members of the Association (at the rate of one pound each)		135/0/0	Balance brought down	99,124/5/11
Balance, being estimated Deficiency		100,089/5/11	Estimated Liabilities	1,100
		£100,224 5s 11d		£100,224 5s 11d

BALANCE SHEET
20 May, 1909.

LIABILITIES			ASSETS		
		£/s/d			£/s/d
Sundry Creditors:			Cash in National Bank	781/14/1	

Estimated amount payable to The Pembroke Urban District Council in respect of a judgment awarded in the King's Bench Division on 24 April 1909	£500/0/0		Cash in hands of Solicitors	24/0/10	805/14/11
Estimated Law Costs, etc.	600/0/0	1,100/0/0	Cash in National Bank on Deposit Receipt, in names of W.M. Murphy and George A. Thompson	302/1/8	
Hely's Limited, secured by Deposit Receipt in the names of W.M. Murphy and George A. Thompson, per contra	302/1/8		Interest on same		0/16/9
Bank of Ireland, Balance of Overdraft		1,203/3/3	Amount payable by members of Association under Clause 7 of the Memorandum of Association		135/0/0
Guarantors:			Estimated Deficiency		100,089/5/11
(1) To Bank: Amounts paid to Bank of Ireland by guarantors	96,630/14/1				
(2) To Association: Amounts paid under direct Guarantees	2,096/19/5	98,727/14/4			
		£101,030 17s 7d			£101,030 17s 7d

Jas. A. Kinnear, PSAA, Chief Accountant and Cashier.
Auditor's Report

We have examined the foregoing Income and Expenditure Account and Balance Sheet, and have obtained all the information and explanations required by us.

Since the formation of the Association we have from time to time examined the Books of the Executive Council, and during the period when the Exhibition was open, a monthly Statement of Receipts and Payments was submitted to us by the Finance Committee, to whom we made reports thereon. We also made a monthly examination and report on the books and accounts kept by Messrs J.C. Lyons & Co., Ltd, as managers of the catering department. These reports contain full information as to the checks adopted with regard to the various sources of income. As regards the expenditure, we examined vouchers for all payments, and satisfied ourselves that same were duly passed by the committee.

Subject to the above-mentioned reports, and subject to the accuracy of the estimated outstanding liabilities, we certify the foregoing Income and Expenditure Account to be correct, and in our opinion the above Balance Sheet is properly drawn up so as to exhibit a true and correct view of the state of the affairs of the Association, according to the best of our information and the explanations given to us, and as shown by the books.

Craig, Gardner & Co., Auditors.
Dublin,
27 May 1909.

SCHEDULE 1

Admissions

	£/s/d	£/s/d
By payment at gates:		
1,115,664 at 1/-	55,783/4/0	
230,006 at 6d	5,750/3/0	
14,156 at 3d	176/19/0	
1,400 at 5/-	350/0/0	
316 at 2/6	39/10/0	
1,361,542	62,099/16/0	
Add cash over amount registered by turnstiles	2/14/8	
	62,102/10/8	

Deduct refunds	2/11/0	
		£62,099 19s 8d
Season tickets:		
Adults: 9,900 at 21/-	10,395/0/0	
2,763 at 10/6	1,450/11/6	
Childs: 821 at 10/6	431/0/6	
438 at 5/3	114/19/6	
13,922	12,391/11/6	
Deduct discount and commission	211/3/9	
		12,180/7/9
Coupon tickets		1,056/1/8½
Railway, steamboat, and miscellaneous tickets		3,644/11/8½
Amount entered in Statement of Income		£78,981 0s 10d

SCHEDULE II

Sideshows and Entertainments

					Gross Drawings	Proportion falling to Exhibition
A	Under Concession:				£/s/d	£/s/d
	Somali Village	25% on			9,601/5/0	2,400/6/6
	Indian Theatre	33⅓% on			2,351/13/2	783/17/9
	Ants and Bees	50% on			415/7/3	207/13/7
	Crystal Maze	25% on			1,101/17/3	275/9/4
	Military Rifle Range	25% on			851/5/0	212/16/3
	Shooting Jungle	33⅓% on			744/11/8	248/3/11
	Nett			15/0/0		
	American Dodger	25% on		63/0/6	78/0/6	15/15/2
	Toft's Hobby Horses	50% on			1,364/19/7	682/9/9
	Toft's Swingboats	50% on			70/17/5	35/8/8
	Baby Incubator, Fixed Payment				2,412/10/3	250/0/0
	Dancing hall	50% on		153/0/0		
	33⅓% on	203/1/6		356/1/6	144/3/10	
					£19,348 8s 7d	£5,256 4s 9d

B	Property of Exhibition:				
	Water chute			7,094/10/9	
	Rivers of Ireland			2,104/11/6	
	Helter-skelter			2,118/18/0	
	Switchback			4,505/4/2	
	Cinematograph Drawings			2,432/5/10	
	Concert Hall Drawings			2,747/3/0	
					21,002/13/3
	Amount entered in Statement of Income				£26,258 18s 0d

SCHEDULE III

Printing and other concessions

	£/s/d
Printing and sale of official catalogues	4,000/0/0
Picture Postcard rights	350/0/0
Palmistry kiosk	100/0/0
Tobacco and cigar sale rights	425/0/0
Liebig extract of Malt Co.	50/0/0
Hat renovating percentage	5/1/5
Model dairy percentage	34/5/10
Automatic machines percentage	587/2/4
Amount entered in Statement of Income	£5,551 9s 7d

SCHEDULE IV

Receipts from Exhibitors

	£/s/d
Electric light and power	4,562/2/10
Storage of empty cases	380/16/0
Water supply	68/16/9
Steam supply	61/10/0
Amount entered in Statement of Income	£5,073 5s 7d

SCHEDULE V

Realisation Account

	£/s/d	£/s/d
Catering Plant:		
Gross receipts	8,245/2/10	
Deduct expenses	155/13/11	
		8,089/8/11
Buildings:		
Gross receipts	7,371/17/2	
Deduct expenses	563/14/4	
		6,808/2/10
Electrical Plant:		
Gross receipts	2,081/14/4	
Deduct expenses	108/16/2	
		1,972/18/2
General Plant:		
Gross receipts	2,123/17/3	
Deduct expenses	100/4/11½	
		2,023/12/3½
Lavatories and Plumbing:		
Gross receipts	742/15/0	
Deduct expenses	30/2/3	
		712/12/9
Grounds:		
Gross receipts	435/15/7	
Deduct expenses	17/17/7	
		417/18/0
Home Industries:		
Gross receipts	185/11/2	
Deduct expenses	7/7/10	
		178/3/4
Amount entered in Statement of Income	£20,202 16s 3½d	

SCHEDULE VI

Miscellaneous Receipts

	£/s/d	£/s/d
Subscriptions		997/0/0
Cloakrooms and lavatories:		
Gross receipts	1,633/16/8½	
Less wages and expenses	752/16/5	
		881/0/3½
Committee members' badges		23/17/0
Picture postcards sold		19/0/0
Sundries		29/7/6½
Amount entered in Statement of Income		£1,950 4s 1d

SCHEDULE VII A

Buildings and Grounds

		£/s/d	£/s/d
A	Buildings:		
	Erection of buildings (Schedule VII A)	118,061/0/3	
	Lavatory fittings and plumbing	3,563/16/2	
	Architects' and Surveyors' fees	1456/5/0	
	Salary, Clerk of Works, etc.	238/17/1	
	Hire of turnstiles	145/15/2	
	Ornaments and vases	50/0/0	
	Ventilation of Art Gallery	72/4/8	
	Sundries	16/4/1	
			123,604/2/5
B	Grounds:		
	Roads and paths	17,106/14/10	
	Drainage	3,660/9/5	
	Fire mains, laying same, and fire fittings	1,223/12/11	
	Salaries and wages	1,045/11/3	
	Plants, shrubs, etc.	786/9/11	
	Painting, flags and decorations	569/3/0	

Bandstand	521/17/7	
Cartage	304/3/6	
Illuminated fountain	269/8/8	
Noticeboards	213/16/7	
Pots, tools, vases, etc.	147/1/0	
Sundry materials	51/13/5	
Restoration of grounds (wages, cartage, and other expenses)	2,100/15/0	
Amount entered in Statement of Expenditure		28,000/17/1
		£151,604 19s 6d

SCHEDULE VII B

Costs of Various Buildings

	£/s/d
Main Entrance block	15,208/19/9
Central Palace and bandstand	33,749/7/8
Palace of Mechanical Arts, Engine Beds, etc.	13,380/0/9
Palace of Fine Arts and additions	7,948/6/6
Palace of Industries	7,991/14/2
Palace Restaurant	6,473/15/8
Catering Offices	4,785/9/3
Executive Offices	1,909/8/3
Irish Industries	2,356/16/2
Do. Hospital (erection only)	93/4/2
Gas Pavilion	2,523/19/8
Herbert Hall	951/12/6
Morehampton Road entrance	1,135/19/2
Tea Room	1,088/13/6
Bars and Canteens (excluding front block)	1,560/15/10
Water chute	3,241/15/5
Packing Case Shed	497/14/9
Rivers of Ireland	2,127/3/1
Lavatory Buildings (Main Entrance block excepted)	791/8/3

Boiler House	1,193/16/1
Cinematograph Hall	489/13/4
Doctor's Walk entrance	227/15/1
Tea Room (near Somali Village)	161/11/6
Ants and Bees	53/2/7
Preliminaries	611/15/2
Lake, Bridges and Temple in Lake	3,676/5/7
Fences, Pay Boxes and additions	1,930/14/9
Model Dairy	279/7/0
Miscellaneous Items	1,620/14/8
Amount entered in Schedule VII	£118,061 0s 3d

SCHEDULE VIII

Catering Department

	£/s/d	£/s/d
Goods	37,971/12/5	
Plant	19,278/3/11	
Salaries and wages	15,647/18/8	
Commission on takings	3,775/13/3	
Printing and stationery	1,033/9/9	
General expenses	606/2/0	
Laundry	624/16/7	
Gas	525/15/4	
Cartage and carriage	479/3/0	
Coal	474/6/8	
Travelling expenses	390/7/6	
Electric light and power	304/8/6	
Signs and noticeboards	154/2/7	
Floral decorations	134/3/0	
Uniforms and costumes	116/6/7	
Fixtures and fittings	85/9/5	
Insurance	66/11/0	
Telephone rent	65/0/0	
Postage	52/17/1	

License	45/17/8	
		81,832/4/11
Less Received from J. Lyons & Co., Ltd		1,000/0/0
Amount entered in Statement of Expenditure		£80,832 4s 11d

SCHEDULE IX

General Administration

		£/s/d	£/s/d
Salaries and Wages:			
Chief Executive Officer	3,704/3/4		
Assistant do.	745/11/6		
General Offices	2,880/4/8		
		7,329/19/6	
Cashiers' and Accountants' Department		873/4/4	
Press Department		318/4/11	
General labour		2,524/7/7	
Admissions and watchmen		1,937/1/10	
Firemen		1,268/6/6	
Ambulance		53/3/9	
Detective and Police services		454/17/10	
			14,759/6/3
Postage, telegrams, cartage, freight, and miscellaneous expenses		2,267/1/1	
Law costs and litigation expenses		2,595/14/6	
Rent, taxes and telephone charges		4,491/3/1	
Advertising		14,531/17/5	
Bank Interest		7,640/1/6	
Printing and stationery		2,817/12/1	
Preliminary expenses		433/9/0	
Reception and ceremonial expenses		1,646/4/4½	
Travelling expenses		696/10/11	
Uniforms		527/0/7	
Insurance		1,241/2/1	
Audit fees		252/0/0	

Compensation for accidents		38/1/6	
General stores		541/2/2½	
Winding-up expenses		236/15/6½	
		39,955/15/10½	
Amount entered in Statement of Expenditure		£54,715 2s 1½d	

SCHEDULE X

Engineer's Department

	£/s/d	£/s/d
Salaries and Wages:		
Engineer	427/0/0	
Laying gas mains	1,868/8/0	
General (Stokers, etc.)	3,657/10/1	
		5,952/18/1
Materials used in electrical installation		3,530/19/11
Plant		7,338/6/11
Hire of lamps, standards, etc.		1,657/1/0
Gas supply		1,644/10/3
Electric current		18/6/3
Hire of machinery		1,505/19/0
Coal		1,126/11/0
Cartage and freight		312/5/1
Water for Lake and general supply		297/5/10
Stationery and sundries		44/5/5
Amount entered in Statement of Expenditure		£23,428 8s 9d

SCHEDULE XI

Music, Entertainments and Attractions

	£/s/d
Bands (per Schedule XI A)	11,220/0/2
Concert Hall Entertainers (per Schedule XI B)	1,631/11/2
Cinematograph, wages and expenses	474/13/5
Fireworks	460/17/6

Illuminations	456/13/4
Musical Directors' fees	427/17/6
Organists' fees	225/15/0
Hire of organ	200/0/0
Wages	166/19/4
Music scores	33/10/9
Scenery	30/0/0
Sundry expenses	125/14/6½
Sideshows, wages, and other running expenses	1,880/5/2
Amount entered in Statement of Expenditure	£17,333/17/10½

SCHEDULE XI A

Bands and Orchestras

Name	Period	Fees	Travelling Expenses	Total
		£/s/d	£/s/d	£/s/d
87th Royal Irish Fusiliers (Faugh-a-Ballaghs)	7½ weeks	766/13/2	1/12/8	768/5/10
Royal Marine Light Infantry (Plymouth)	2 weeks	480/0/0	107/11/10	587/11/10
1st Gordon Highlanders	1 week	116/13/4	18/3/11	134/17/3
Royal Marines (Chatham)	2 weeks	540/0/0	91/13/2	631/13/2
2nd Life Guards	2 weeks	460/0/0	73/9/9	533/9/9
Royal Engineers (Chatham)	2 weeks	476/13/4	91/8/9	568/2/1
1st Royal Berkshire	1 week	168/0/0		168/0/0
Coldstream Guards	3 weeks	832/10/0	167/5/7	999/15/7
Royal Irish Constabulary	1 week	131/16/0		131/16/0
15th Canadian Light Horse	2 weeks	400/0/0		400/0/0
19th Hussars (Princess of Wales Own)	1 wk, 3 days	150/0/0		150/0/0
Royal Marines (Portsmouth)	2 weeks	554/8/0	93/6/3	647/14/3

Royal Marine Light Infantry (Plymouth)	2 weeks	360/0/0	86/8/3	446/8/3
HM Royal Horse Guards (Blues)	2 weeks	462/0/0	84/11/3	546/11/3
Grenadier Guards	2 weeks	630/0/0	84/11/3	714/11/3
Royal Artillery (Woolwich)	2 weeks	550/0/0	87/16/3	637/16/3
4th Royal Dublin Fusiliers	3 wks, 2 days	125/10/0		125/10/0
2nd Royal Dublin Fusiliers (HM 103rd)	1 week	60/0/0	18/15/5	78/15/0
2nd Essex Regt (Pompadours)	1 wk, 1 day	98/0/0		98/0/0
Ireland's Own Band	4 days	34/0/0		34/0/0
1st Worcestershire	2 weeks	29/6/0		29/6/0
1st Cameron Highlanders	1 day	15/15/0		15/15/0
Sarsfield Prize Band (Limerick)	1 day	11/3/0		11/3/0
Dublin Operative Bakers' Band	1 day	5/5/0		5/5/0
York Street Workmen's Club Band	1 day	5/5/0		5/5/0
Dublin Total Abstinence Workingmen's Band	1 day	5/0/0		5/0/0
Herr Kandt's Orchestra	6 weeks	824/0/6	66/9/0	890/9/6
Herr Moritz Wurm's Viennese Blue	4 weeks	600/0/0	66/9/0	666/9/0
Casino Orchestra (Herr Von Leer)	2 weeks	210/0/0	33/4/6	243/4/6
Austro-Hungarian Orchestra	2 weeks	280/0/0	33/4/6	313/4/6
De-long's Orchestra	1 week	165/0/0		165/0/0
Grandpierre Orchestra	19 weeks	322/10/0		322/10/0
Tattoos (fees & expenses)		144/10/6		144/10/6
	£10,002/15/10	£1,217/4/4		
Amount entered in Schedule XI				£11,220/0/2

SCHEDULE XI B

Concert Hall, Entertainers, etc.

	£ s d
Tyrolese Troupe	90/0/0
Yo-San Troupe	60/0/0
Two Daniels	15/0/0
A Ba Bé	20/0/0
Arthur Helmore	21/0/0
Virginia Serenaders	40/0/0
Souasa Arab Troupe	45/0/0
Sabots	45/0/0
The Wheelers	50/0/0
The Melody Makers	40/0/0
Don Pedro	46/5/0
Harrison Hill	31/10/0
Virginia Minstrels	65/0/0
Estrella	10/0/0
Grandpierre	32/0/0
New Philharmonic Society	40/4/0
Maiden City Choir	50/0/0
Wm. Ludwig (proportion of takings)	368/7/0
H. Loreto	25/0/0
Griffith Humphreys ('The Motorists')	45/0/0
Dr G. Sinclair (Special Organ Recitals)	42/0/0
Alexandroff Troupe	90/0/0
Philharmonic Society	8/8/0
L. Street	7/0/0
O'Phelan (Irish Piper)	3/0/0
Jack Vincent (Edeophonist)	12/12/0
Leipzig	70/0/0
Edgar Warwick, 'The Tatlers'	45/0/0
George Grossmith	157/10/0
Madame Cora	5/12/2
Charles Kelly	7/7/0

Charles Cosgrave	6/6/0
Madame Heller (Irish Ladies' Choir)	12/1/0
Sundries	4/9/0
Faugh-a-Ballagh's Concert	21/0/0
	1,631/11/2
Amount entered in Schedule XI	£1,631 11s 2d

SCHEDULE XII

Fine Arts Section

	£/s/d	£/s/d
Collection, delivery and carriage of pictures, etc.		2,839/2/2
Insurance		2,084/5/3
Photographic Section expenses		110/8/2
Wages		407/0/3
Rent and storage		95/0/0
Canvas, muslin, etc.		596/19/10
Fees		50/0/0
Travelling expenses		226/18/11
Sundries – London Committee		75/13/5
Sundries – Dublin Committee		16/9/6
Claims for damaged pictures, etc.	299/1/6	
Less recovered from Insurance Co.	270/12/9	
		28/8/9
Postage		17/11/3
Printing and stationery		89/19/9
Amount entered in Statement of Expenditure		£6,637 17s 3d

SCHEDULE XIII

Historical Section

	£/s/d
Travelling expenses	578/6/9
London Section expenses	10/0/0

Wages	73/9/7
Freight, packing, etc.	253/7/6
Repairs to objects	23/14/6
Show cases	21/11/8
Honorarium	100/0/0
Paris office expenses	6/11/6
Storage	30/0/0
Sundries	71/0/3½
Amount entered in Statement of Expenditure	£1,168 1s 9½d

SCHEDULE XIV

Home Industries Section

	£/s/d	£/s/d
Salaries and wages	1,077/9/8	
Cases, lining same, etc.	1,132/9/8	
Office fittings	134/6/5	
Printing and stationery	106/15/8	
Installing machinery and repairs	105/14/10	
Decorations and painting	101/0/4	
Electrical installation, and current for light and power	362/10/1	
Travelling expenses	81/0/11	
Sundry expenses	79/6/11	
Rents	10/10/0	
Postage	28/19/7	
Carriage	27/9/11	
Insurance	43/5/6	
Pottery exhibit	39/11/2	
Tobacco exhibit	16/19/11	
Weaving requisites	75/5/8	
Petrol lighting	10/0/0	
		3,432/16/3
Less grants:		

Department of Agriculture	2,000/0/0	
Congested Districts Board	250/0/0	2,250/0/0
Amount entered in Statement of Expenditure		£1,182 16s 3d

SCHEDULE XV

Plant, Fittings and Office Furniture

	£/s/d
Chairs	1,169/12/9
Switchback and Helter-skelter	1,029/5/6
Sundry furnishings	520/10/5
Lifts (Water chute)	305/0/0
Office furniture	186/10/9
Slot locks	76/0/10
Band music stands	45/18/9
Steel rails, etc.	32/18/1
Ladders and trucks	32/4/6
Sundries	11/6/9
Amount entered in Statement of Expenditure	£3,409 8s 4d

IRISH INTERNATIONAL EXHIBITION WINDING-UP MEETING

Thursday 20 May 1909

The following extracts are taken from the Dublin papers:

The purpose for which the Irish International Exhibition (Incorporated) was formed having been fulfilled, it was decided, at an extraordinary general meeting of the members, held on Thursday, 20 May 1909, in the offices of Messrs Casey, Clay and Collins, Solicitors, that the Association be wound up voluntarily.

Liquidators were appointed to give effect to the resolution. Mr Wm. M. Murphy, Vice-President of the Association, presided. The chairman said:

This meeting is more or less of a formal character, and it is called in order to comply with the 41st clause of the Articles of Association, which states that the Association shall wind-up voluntarily as soon as convenient after the fulfilment of the purpose for which it is established. The meeting to-day is a meeting of the members of the

Association, and I think it is the second meeting of the members of the Association ever held. Members are distinguished by the Articles of Association as gentlemen who have either subscribed £10 or guaranteed £50 and who have intimated their desire to become members of the Association, and I should like to inform you that the liability is not a heavy one, but they are each individually liable for £1 in the winding-up if anyone comes to demand it from them. I do not know if that will cheer them up very much, but that is the last limit of their liability – £1 for each member. I might give a short history of the undertaking.

As far as dates are concerned, the record is that the Company was incorporated on 16 July 1904, for the purpose of carrying out the Exhibition. On the 27 June 1905, we signed the lease of the site at Herbert Park, and we got that lease for three years. We entered into a contract for building on 19 February 1906. The Exhibition was opened on 4 May 1907, and it closed on 9 November 1907.

On the close of the Exhibition it was open to us, under the Articles of Association, to hold this meeting, and wind-up the Association and appoint a liquidator, but the members of the Finance Committee, who had done most of the work in organising the Exhibition and carrying it through, thought they could themselves more economically and better realise the property than if they handed it over to a professional liquidator, and I think the result justified that anticipation.

The members of the committee, since the close of the Exhibition, have held no fewer than fifty meetings, and, in addition to that, individual members of the committee have given a considerable amount of time and attention to the realisation of the property. The result of the realisation was that we received £20,202 16s 3½d. That realisation was not carried out without a great deal of thought and trouble and management. It would have been very easy to sacrifice the place by selling it wholesale to the highest bidder, but we went into every detail most carefully, and had a series of auctions spreading over the best part of six months, and we realised, I think, between saving of expenses, and the larger sum that we got for the property, more than would have been received if the matter had been handed over to a professional liquidator – between £5,000 and £10,000. Mr Dennehy is editing, and it will be published, a Record of the Exhibition, which will give a complete statement of the accounts.

We cannot give you an absolutely final statement to-day, because we have still pending a question of costs in connection with the recent action by the Pembroke Council against the Company. The damages they got were £500, having claimed £11,000, and they put us to the expense of £600 or £700 in defending the action, and their own costs are, I think, nearly as much. I think it is right to tell the members that the action of the Pembroke Council was forced on the Company, and that we did not allow it to go on without making efforts to settle it, and that we thought we would be doing what was fair to the council and saving the Association money by offering them £1,000. We did this, and Sir Robert Gardner tried to induce them to accept it, but the majority of the council indignantly refused to take it. They have now got a verdict for £500. Their action has delayed the winding-up of our affairs unduly.

The total expenditure we incurred from the beginning was £340,312 16s 9d, and our receipts were £241,461 15s 5d, the balance being a deficit of £98,851.

The chairman then expressed thanks to the Bank of Ireland and its officials, and said that from first to last they had treated the Exhibition Company in the most generous manner.

Dealing with the Exhibition year he said:

It was a boom year in the trade of the city. Evidence of that is to be found in the speeches of the Chairmen at meetings of every public carrying company or trading company held this year. In relation to the accounts for the year 1908 nearly one and all apologised for the falling-off in profits, owing it to the fact that the previous year – 1907 – had been an exceptionally good year.

Adverting back to the question of the Pembroke Council – I do not know that it is worth while really going back – but we surrendered the Park on 29 June 1908, and at that time we were in the process of completing the work, which was ultimately estimated by a jury to be worth £500. We asked for two or three weeks to be allowed to carry it out, but they refused to do so. Our letter to Mr Manly stated:

Being desirous of giving up possession immediately, the Association employed a large number of men to expedite the clearance, and, as far as possible, to put the grounds into a reasonable condition and, although, as stated in my previous letter, the Association will deliver up possession on Monday, the 29th inst., at twelve o'clock, they propose, unless your committee objects to their so doing, to retain the staff of workmen to continue the clearance and put the grounds in such order as under the circumstances the Association can be reasonably expected to do. I am, however, to distinctly intimate that the Association will not undertake any liability or obligation as to possession, rent or otherwise after the lease expires.

Of course, if we passed that day without surrendering the property, we would be liable for another £1,000 for rent. The effect of our proposal was that, while we should not be liable for rent, we would continue to keep our workmen there and complete the restoration of the Park. They refused to take possession, and we drew our men away, and left the place to them. The position we are in now is this. We have, in the course of the last fifteen or sixteen months since the Exhibition closed, applied ourselves to clearing off all the liabilities of the Exhibition and realising the assets. We have cleared off every liability of every kind and form, and we have provided, as far as we know, for expenditure, such as the cost of the publication of the Record, which will be required in the future, and we have a small sum left over, against which the Bank, of course, will have a claim, as well as the Pembroke Council.

Mr James Talbot-Power proposed that, 'The purpose for which the Association was formed having been fulfilled, it is hereby resolved that the Association be wound up voluntarily.'

Alderman Cotton seconded the resolution, which was unanimously adopted. Mr Thomas Davy proposed, 'That Col. Arthur H. Courtenay, CB, DL; Mr Wm. M. Murphy, JP; Mr Robert Booth, JP; Mr R.S. Tresilian, and Mr W.F. Dennehy be appointed liquidators for such winding-up.' Mr Ralph Smalley seconded.

The chairman, in putting the resolution, said:

The liquidators would be too numerous if we included all those who attended the meetings of the committee, and who have had the realisation and winding-up of this thing for the last eighteen months, and nothing could exceed the attention given by these gentlemen, but perhaps those we have named have been the most regular attendants at the various meetings of the committee – Colonel Courtenay, Mr Booth, and Mr Tresilian. The whole cost paid out, excluding the legal expenses – for running the Association – from the time of winding-up the Exhibition until now – was £236, and that was very moderate.

(Mr Hatte) Did that include everything?

(The chairman) Yes, it included everything – clerical and office staff, from the time of the closing of the Exhibition. I suppose it is public knowledge that the Pembroke Council have filed a petition to wind up the Company. Of course, it means wasting more money to themselves, and probably to us also.

The resolution was unanimously adopted. Colonel Courtenay, in proposing a vote of thanks to Mr Murphy for his conduct in the chair, said:

We all know the interest he has taken in the welfare of the Exhibition, and, having had the pleasure of serving with him on this committee for the past year, I can say I never met anyone who has taken greater interest or done more or given more of his time for our welfare than Mr Murphy.

Mr Lee seconded the motion, and said the only member of the Pembroke Council that came out of the recent action with any degree of credit was Sir Robert Gardner. He was delighted to see the sensible, business-like way in which Sir Robert recommended his council to act in connection with the Exhibition ('hear, hear'). The motion was adopted.

The chairman, in returning thanks, said:

I went into this thing first as a labour of love, and continued in it, I am afraid, more or less in a fighting spirit, when it was attacked, and I thought that at all events I would see it decently interred, and that it got proper obsequies, and I stuck to it all through. Of course, at the time the Exhibition was over it was urged that we ought to appoint a liquidator, and it would save us a great deal of trouble and worry, but I foresaw that there would be points constantly arising of a legal and technical character, and I believed that those things would be less costly dealt with by a committee than by a liquidator.

STATUTORY MEETING OF CREDITORS

Friday 4 June 1909

(From the Dublin papers.)
On Friday 4 June 1909, a meeting of the creditors of the Irish International Exhibition Company (Incorporated) was held at the Central Hall, 12 Westmoreland Street, Dublin.

On the motion of Col. Arthur H. Courtenay, Mr William M. Murphy took the Chair.

Mr W.F. Dennehy said the meeting was called in pursuance of the following notice:

> Notice is hereby given, pursuant to Section 188 (1) of the Companies (Consolidation) Act, 1908, that a meeting of creditors of the Company (The Irish International Exhibition, Incorporated) will be held at the Central Hall, 12 Westmoreland Street, Dublin, on Friday the 4th day of June, 1909, at twelve o'clock noon.
>
> Dated this 21st day of May 1909,
> ARTHUR H. COURTENAY, COL.
> W.M. MURPHY
> ROBERT BOOTH
> R.S. TRESILIAN
> W.F. DENNEHY
> (liquidators)

The chairman: A meeting of the members of the Association of the Irish International Exhibition (Incorporated) was held on 20 May, at which a resolution appointing the gentlemen whose names are mentioned in the notice, as liquidators, to wind up the Company voluntarily was adopted. The purpose of the Company having been effected – that is to say, the Exhibition having been held, its proceedings and accounts practically wound up, the following gentlemen were appointed liquidators of the Company: Arthur H. Courtenay, Col.; W.M. Murphy, Robert Booth, R.S. Tresilian, and W.F. Dennehy. In pursuance of the provisions of the Acts of Parliament relating to limited companies, it was necessary for the liquidators to call a meeting of the creditors, and this meeting was accordingly called in pursuance of the 188th Section of the Act.

The purpose of the meeting is that the creditors might – if they think fit – appoint an additional liquidator or a Committee of Inspection. If anyone present is of the opinion that the liquidators are not sufficiently numerous, he can move to have an additional one appointed, or to have a Committee of Inspection.

If you are satisfied to allow the liquidation to proceed in the hands of the liquidators already appointed, and if you think they will deal properly with the assets, which are now of exceedingly small dimensions, a resolution to that effect will be in order. I am glad to say that outside the money due by the guarantors to the bank, the amount at present due to creditors is very small – in fact, there is only one creditor, the Pembroke Urban Council. If anyone present has a resolution to propose in connection with this matter, I will receive it, or if you are prepared to allow the liquidation to go on in the hands of the present liquidators, I will receive a resolution to that effect.

Mr Gee, of Messrs Millar & Beatty's, proposed, and Mr O'Rourke, of Messrs Forde & Co., seconded, the following resolution, which was carried unanimously, 'That the creditors determine that no application shall be made to the Court for the appointment of any person as liquidator either in the place of, or jointly with the liquidators already appointed, or for the appointment of a Committee of Inspection'.

(Mr Gee) I consider the gentlemen whose names are returned on this sheet as liquidators are quite capable of dealing properly with the assets of this Association.

(The chairman) There is a petition being presented by the Pembroke Council to wind up the Company compulsorily, and the action of the committee in proceeding with the winding-up resolutions are more or less forced on them by the attitude of the Pembroke Council. For the voluntary liquidation we got the consents signed by the guarantors – sixty-four in number – who have paid up £45,226, while the Pembroke Council's petition to wind-up is in respect of £500 damages and costs. The accounts of the Association have been all examined and audited by Messrs Craig, Gardner, & Co., and have been kept all through by Mr Kinnear's firm. The following is the Report of the Auditors, who have examined the accounts from time to time:

We have examined the foregoing Income and Expenditure Account and Balance Sheet, and have obtained all information and explanations required by us.

Since the formation of the Association we have from time to time examined the books of the Executive Council, and during the period that the Exhibition was open, a monthly statement of receipts and payments was submitted to us by the Finance Committee, to whom we made reports throughout. We also made a monthly examination and report on the books and accounts kept by Messrs J.C. Lyons & Co., as managers of the catering department. Their reports contain full information as to the checks adopted with regard to the full sources of income. As regards the expenditure we examined vouchers for all payments, and satisfied ourselves that same were duly passed by the committee. Subject to the above-mentioned reports, and subject to the accuracy of the estimated outstanding liabilities, we certify the foregoing Income and Expenditure Account to be correct, and in our opinion the above Balance Sheet is properly drawn up so as to exhibit a true and correct view of the state of the affairs of the Association according to the best of our information, and the explanations given to us, and as shown by the books.

CRAIG, GARDNER & CO.,
Auditors.

I might add, [continued the chairman] that all the accounts were kept throughout the entire undertaking – both before and after the Exhibition – by the firm of Messrs J.A. Kinnear & Co., with the greatest credit to Mr Kinnear and to his staff. I have had a good deal of experience in the keeping of accounts relating to large undertakings, and I cannot say that I have ever seen accounts kept more carefully and accurately, or where less leakage has taken place, than, in this case ('hear, hear').

This concluded the business and the meeting terminated.

LIQUIDATORS' ACCOUNT

Summary of the Liquidators' Receipts and Payments from 20 may 1909 to 31 August 1909

		RECEIPTS				PAYMENTS
	£/s/d	£/s/d		£/s/d	£/s/d
To Cash in National Bank, College Green, on Current Account	781/14/1		By Pembroke Urban District Council, payment in full discharge of judgment and costs		740/0/0
To Cash in Hands of Solicitors	24/0/10		Hely's Ltd, Deposit Receipt as at contra uplifted	302/1/8	
		805/14/11			

Cash in National Bank, on Deposit Receipt in the names of Wm. M. Murphy and Geo. A. Thompson as per contra	302/1/8		Accountant's fees, preparing final accounts, schedules and Balance Sheet	15/0/0
Interest on above	0/16/9		Solicitor's charges and Counsel's fees	77/6/8
Cash received from Bank of Ireland	50/0/0		Advertisements in local papers, re statutory meeting, printing and sundry expenses	15/9/4
Balance in Hands to meet advertising and incidental expense				8/15/8
		856/11/8		856/11/8

ARTHUR H. COURTENAY, COL., CB,
W.M. MURPHY
ROBERT BOOTH
R.S. TRESILIAN
W.F. DENNEHY
Liquidators.